Reader's Digest

CELEBRATION *of* CHRISTMAS

Stories, Crafts and Recipes

Reader's Digest

The Reader's Digest Association, Inc.
Pleasantville, New York • Montreal • London • Sydney

Reader's Digest

CELEBRATION *of* CHRISTMAS
Stories, Crafts and Recipes

Conceived and designed by
The Reader's Digest Association (Canada) Limited

Reader's Digest Books and Home Entertainment, Montreal
Senior Editor/Project Leader: Andrew Byers
Director, Music Products Development: Nancy Hart
Designer: Cécile Germain
Production Manager: Holger Lorenzen
Production Coordinator: Susan Wong

Vice President: Deirdre Gilbert
Art Director: John McGuffie

Contributors
Designer: Gillian Stead
Copy Editor: Joseph Marchetti

ISBN 0-88850-755-0

Printed in Canada
02 03 04 05 / 5 4 3 2 1

Table of Contents

Holiday Memories

RECAPTURE THE CHRISTMAS SPIRIT THROUGH
THE REALM OF PERSONAL RECOLLECTION

Grandma Mollie and Grandpa in front of their house

A Family Christmas

By Jessamyn West

The magazines lie side by side on the coffee table. One has given its space to an examination of the possibility of a nuclear holocaust. The second, this being the season when Christmas is celebrated, is filled with the memories of those who entered this world before such words had come into use.

I am such a one. Not only to a world that had no use for these words, but to a region, southern Indiana, that loved words and knew how to use them.

Near the farm where I was born were towns with names like "Gnaw Bone," "Bean Blossom," "Stony Lonesome," "Maple Grove." Writers Booth Tarkington and Lew Wallace, who wrote Ben Hur, grew up in nearby counties. Christmas celebrations in one-room schoolhouses from the Atlantic to the Pacific heard the recitation of Christmas verse written by Indiana poet James Whitcomb Riley.

There was less poetry heard in my grandparents' farmhouse, where I spent my first five Christmases; but the Christmases celebrated there were not quiet, either. There were reasons this was so.

First, those meeting for the celebration, though frequently related, often lived far apart. Some had not seen each other for years. They came from as far away as Kansas or Kentucky. They arrived by spring-wagon or surrey as there was no train into town. Since they were celebrating not only the birth of their Savior but the meeting after long absence of brothers and sisters, of mothers and sons, the shouts of cousins from Kansas and the softer greetings of brothers-in-law from Kentucky could be heard. Family ties had brought them to that one white farmhouse.

Children, of course, were the chief source of Christmas sounds. In later years one of those farmhouse children, remembering his earliest Christmases, wrote of his father:

> Pa, he's good to all of us
> All the time; but when
> Ever' time it's Christmas,
> He's as good again!
>
> 'Side our toys and candy,
> Ever' Christmas he
> Gives us all a quarter,
> Certain as can be!

Candy and toys and quarters! Christmas has changed, and in many ways the Christmases of my childhood were unlike the ones we celebrate now. Much that characterizes a Christmas today had not yet reached Jennings County, Indiana, during the first decade of this century. Christmas trees were not popular there as they were in England where Queen Victoria had brought them from the dark German forests of her bridegroom. Why should they be? The pioneers had spent two centuries cutting down similar trees that impeded their passage across the continent. Why should they now fill a parlour with brothers of the departed? At my grandparents' home it was certainly not done. The birth of Christ was not celebrated by the death of a tree.

This was the least of that household's peculiarities. My grandfather, a Quaker of long standing, played the accordion. His mother, a widow who shared his home, was a Quaker minister. Female preachers were not novelties to the Quakers; but a preacher whose son played the accordion was.

Children, of course, were the chief source of Christmas sounds.

It was easy in those days to give children something they didn't have.

In addition to this, Grandpa had married an Irish girl. "Marrying out of Meeting" was not approved in those days. Quaker married Quaker. Marrying a non-Quaker Irish girl was as unconventional as accordion playing. Members of that sect believed that music stirred up the baser passion. But one look at Mary Frances Cavanagh was so stirring music was unnecessary. One look at the black hair, blue eyes, pink cheeks, made marriage, "in Meeting" or out, desirable.

Known as "Mollie" to her husband's family, and later "Grandma" to us, she seemed to have brought Christmas with her into that farmhouse. Grandma didn't transport trees from Ireland, but she did transform the house with loops of crinkled crepe paper. Pictures still remain of the long Christmas dinner table under a pagoda-like conical roof of Grandma's crepe paper attached to the kerosene lamp suspended from the ceiling.

Before the food was set forth under Grandma's crepe paper pagoda, the Christmas gifts were distributed. This was at an early hour, without the benefit of trees or stockings hung at the fireplace. The hour was early to keep the children quiet. Once the toys, the candy, and possibly the quarters were in the children's hands, there was nothing more for them to scream about.

The gifts were homemade, not store-bought, and often they were the same year after year. Aunt Allie, for example, always made bib aprons for the girls. For the boys, she knitted mittens. Grown women received pot holders, large and fancy with appliqués of farm vegetables or animals. No one complained of the monotony. There was none. Calico for aprons came in innumerable colors and designs. Mittens sometimes had fingers, sometimes did not. Christmas cards were not yet used. People still wrote letters.

It was easy in those days to give children something they didn't have. Almost any toy was magical then—clothespin dolls and balls made by winding string around a core of rubber. And a thread spool rigged up so that you could knit with it; or a homemade Indian suit of fringed khaki with an Indian bonnet, likewise homemade, of mixed Rhode Island Red and Plymouth Rock feathers.

My own mother liked to cook, and the best gift you could give her was to eat a lot of what she had provided. She often made a fondant at Christmas that she called "heavenly hash." She made it by the dishpanful, Papa pouring the hot syrup over the beaten whites of eggs while she stirred.

She made plum puddings that she steamed in one-pound Hills Brothers coffee cans; and while others may think of Christmas red as the red of holly berries, I think of it as the red of Hills Brothers coffee cans. She made plum puddings as she made everything—in bulk—so that if you were starved for plum pudding, you could sit down and eat a whole one without worrying about being selfish.

She made candied orange peel—crisp, sweet-bitter—by the crockful. She candied big English walnut halves, and fried others in butter and salted them in such quantities that by December twenty-seventh or twenty-eighth no one wanted to see another English walnut.

It was better for her to concoct her Christmas sweets about the day before Christmas. Once, trying to be forehanded (which didn't come naturally to her), she bought a five-pound bucket of store candy a couple of weeks before Christmas. Immediately after that she began saying, "Oh, children, shut your eyes. I think I hear Santa Claus's reindeer on the roof." We would close our eyes, and sure enough, when we opened them Santa had been there, leaving double handfuls of gumdrops and peppermint sticks and licorice whips. Santa just couldn't resist these premature visits— and by the time Christmas arrived he had run out of candy.

After the presents had been distributed, the dinner, which was Grandma's Christmas contribution, was put on the table. Dinner alone of our Christmas ritual differed from that of the neighboring farms where chicken was the meat dish. This was the result of the presence at the table of two women who had learned their cooking miles away in Kansas and Ireland. In Ireland a meat pie in which chicken might be included was served. Kansas brought to the feast what was portable: ham. Grandma prepared what was accepted as the ideal accompaniment of ham: candied sweet potatoes. Grandpa's mother's contribution was the result of fifty years of practice in making: a fruitcake the size of the washbowl that held the pitcher of water in each bedroom.

Christmas afternoons at Grandma Mollie's were well organized. While the young women cleared the tables, the children and older women examined the presents—their own and those of others. My cousin Ben who, along with my sister Lydia, said he liked the Fourth of July more than Christmas, demonstrated this by swinging the rag doll I had been given so close to the base-burner that you could smell her petticoats scorching. He said she was a Tory. After a trip to the woodshed with his father, Ben came back, like my doll, a hundred percent Yankee.

She made candied orange peel—crisp, sweet-bitter—by the crockful.

She wanted

snow.

Nothing

was so

Christmassy

as snow.

For Grandma Mollie, however, the purpose of Christmas had little to do with eating and gift giving. Such activities were in no way evil, but they were no more particularly suited for December twenty-fifth than for May first.

The word for Christmas was love. There were many acts of love, and gift giving could be one of them. The toys, the candy, even the quarters, made their appearance, but we were never permitted to forget that the purpose of Christmas was to celebrate the birth of Jesus in the hearts of those who loved Him.

Love comes from the heart and can best be made known by language. Grandma Mollie, with an Irishwoman's belief that we exist more fully when we let others know by the words we use what lies at our heart's core, initiated Christmas afternoons of talk. The talk could be spontaneous; could be the repetition of a poet's words; could be one's memory of words spoken by a forebear long departed the world.

My mother was always the first to be called on. She always repeated the same verse: a reminder to herself, I always felt, of our human limitations in the sight of God.

I know not where His islands lift
Their fronded palms in air;
I only know I cannot drift
Beyond His love and care.

Grandpa knew an accordion piece sufficiently religious to justify its being played on Christmas Day. It was funny, too—called "The Preacher and the Bear." The preacher's presence made the song suitable for the occasion; and the bear, who chased the preacher up a tree but never caught him, provided the excitement.

Could a child who had a mother and a grandmother and a great-grandmother, a rag doll (petticoat slightly scorched), a grandfather who knew a song about a preacher who was chased by a bear, want anything more? This one could. She wanted snow. Nothing was so Christmassy as snow. She had experienced one Christmas when the corncrib was whiter than an Eskimo igloo, when an uncle's whisker had gone from cinnamon to salt-and-pepper.

Most of the objects, songs, poems, associated with Christmas mentioned snow: reindeer and Santa Claus and stockings before the fireplace and sleds and holly seemed materially to belong to snow country. Did Jesus ever see

snow? Southern Indiana was not always snowless, of course. But the Christmas I remember best at Grandma's was.

William Dean Howells characterized the four seasons thus: "We speak of the 'fulness of spring, the height of summer, the heart of autumn and the dead of winter.'" To my mind, there is no "dead of winter" when the ground sparkles with a covering of snow, but it really did exist the Christmases I spent at Grandma's. A sky the color of a cast-iron skillet; leafless trees; a steady fire in the kitchen stove and living-room grate.

Before the journeys home were started, the mittens Aunt Allie had knitted were pulled onto hands already turning blue. Those who lived not too far distant drank their cider and ate their fruitcake early so that their journey wouldn't keep them traveling all night. Those who did live at a distance spent the night, either at Grandma Mollie's or with relatives nearby.

After the travelers had departed, the food had been eaten and Grandma Mollie's program had been completed, those who were spending the night talked on quietly; first of the day that was ending, then of former Christmases when those we did not know had been present. Grandpa's mother, the preacher, told us that when she was young, the birth of the little Jewish child who saved us was remembered with more prayer than was the custom nowadays.

Jessamyn West at lower left, aged five

"Why," said she, "there's so much hullabaloo now you can't tell whether it's July fourth or December twenty-fifth that's being celebrated."

No one was sure whether her words were directed to her son with his accordion or to Ben and Lydia, their red faces betraying their preference.

"Grandmother," her daughter-in-law said, "we haven't come to firecrackers yet for the twenty-fifth."

"Praise be," said Grandmother. "Nor hard cider."

Maybe Ben and Lydia really did prefer the Fourth of July; but for everyone else celebrating Christmas at Grandma Mollie's, there was a heart-warmth no other holiday ever produced. And the heart-warmth for Ben and Lydia has increased with the years. I know. We talk of it often.

No, no other holiday, especially not the Fourth of July with its firecracker imitation of gunfire, is comparable to the day when wise men and shepherds followed the shine of a star which led them to a crib where they learned that God is love.

We still believe it. And on Christmas Day we try to practice it.

Conversation About Christmas

by Dylan Thomas

Small Boy. Years and years ago, when you were a boy . . .

Self. When there were wolves in Wales, and birds the colour of red-flannel petticoats whisked past the harp-shaped hills, when we sang and wallowed all night and day in caves that smelt like Sunday afternoons in damp front farmhouse parlours, and chased, with the jawbones of deacons, the English and the bears . . .

Small Boy. You are not so old as Mr. Benyon Number Twenty-Two who can remember when there were no motors. Years and years ago, when you were a boy . . .

Self. Oh, before the motor even, before the wheel, before the duchess-faced horse, when we rode the daft and happy hills bare-back . . .

Small Boy. You're not so daft as Mrs. Griffiths up the street, who says she puts her ear under the water in the reservoir and listens to the fish talk Welsh. When you were a boy, what was Christmas like?

Self. It snowed.

Small Boy. It snowed last year, too. I made a snowman and my brother

knocked it down and I knocked my brother down and then we had tea.

Self. But that was not the same snow. Our snow was not only shaken in whitewash buckets down the sky, I think it came shawling out of the ground and swam and drifted out of the arms and hands and bodies of the trees; snow grew overnight on the roofs of the houses like a pure and grandfather moss, minutely ivied the walls, and settled on the postman, opening the gate, like a dumb, numb thunderstorm of white torn Christmas cards.

Small Boy. Where there postmen, then, too?

Self. With sprinkling eyes and wind cherried noses, on spread, frozen feet they crunched up to the doors and mittened on them manfully. But all that the children could hear was a ringing of bells.

Small Boy. You mean that the postman went rat-a-tat-tat and the doors rang?

Self. The bells that the children could hear were inside them.

Small Boy. I only hear thunder sometimes, never bells.

Self. There were church bells, too.

Small Boy. Inside them?

Self. No, no, no, in the bat-black, snow-white belfries, tugged by bishops and storks. And they rang their tidings over the bandaged town, over the frozen foam of the powder and ice-cream hills, over the crackling sea. It seemed that all the churches boomed, for joy, under my window; and the weathercocks crew for Christmas, on our fence.

Small Boy. Get back to the postmen.

Self. They were just ordinary postmen, fond of walking, and dogs, and Christmas, and the snow. They knocked on the doors with blue knuckles . . .

Small Boy. Ours has got a black knocker . . .

Self. And then they stood on the white welcome mat in the little, drifted porches, and clapped their hands together, and huffed and puffed, making ghosts with their breath, and jogged from foot to foot like small boys wanting to go out.

Small Boy. And then the Presents?

Self. And then the Presents, after the Christmas box. And the cold postman, with a rose on his button-nose, tingled down the teatray-slithered run of the chilly glinting hill. He went in his ice-bound boots like a man on fishmonger's slabs. He wagged his bag like a frozen camel's hump, dizzily turned the corner on one foot, and by God, he was gone.

I would stay awake all the moonlit, snowlit night to hear the roof-alighting reindeer . . .

Small Boy. Get back to the Presents.

Self. There were the Useful Presents: engulfing mufflers of the old coach days, and mittens made for giant sloths; zebra scarves of a substance like silky gum that could be tug-o'-warred down to the goloshes; blinding tam-o'-shanters like patchwork tea-cozies, and bunny-scutted busbies and balaclavas for victims of head-shrinking tribes; from aunts who always wore wool next to the skin, there were moustached and rasping vests that made you wonder why the aunties had any skin left at all; and once I had a little crocheted nose-bag from an aunt now, alas, no longer whinnying with us. And pictureless books in which small boys, though warned, with quotations, not to, *would* skate on Farmer Garge's pond, and did, and drowned; and books that told me everything about the wasp, except why.

Small Boy. Get on to the Useless Presents.

Self. On Christmas Eve I hung at the foot of my bed Bessie Bunter's black stocking, and always, I said, I would stay awake all the moonlit, snowlit night to hear the roof-alighting reindeer and see the hollied boot descend through soot. But soon the sand of the snow drifted into my eyes, and, though I stared towards the fireplace and around the flickering room where the black sack-like stocking hung, I was asleep before the chimney trembled and the room was red and white with Christmas. But in the morning, though no snow melted on the bedroom floor, the stocking bulged and brimmed: press it, it squeaked like a mouse-in-a-box; it smelt of tangerine; a furry arm lolled over, like the arm of a kangeroo out of its mother's belly; squeeze it hard in the middle, and something squelched; squeeze it again— squelch again. Look out of the frost-scribbled window: on the great loneliness of the small hill, a blackbird was silent in the snow.

Small Boy. Where there any sweets?

Self. Of course there were sweets. It was the marshmallows that squelched. Hardboileds, toffee, fudge and allsorts, crunches, cracknels, humbugs, glaciers, and marzipan and butterwelsh for the Welsh. And troops of bright tin soldiers who, if they would not fight, could always run. And Snakes-and-Families and Happy Ladders. And Easy Hobbi-Games for Little Engineers, complete with Instructions. Oh, easy for Leonardo! And a whistle to make the dogs bark to wake up the old man next door to make him beat on the wall with his stick to shake our picture off the wall. And a packet of cigarettes: you put one in your mouth and you stood at the corner of the street and you waited for hours, in vain, for an old lady to scold you for smoking a cigarette and then, with a smirk, you ate it. And, last of all, in the toe of the stocking, sixpence like a silver corn. And then downstairs for breakfast under the balloons!

Small Boy. Were there Uncles, like in our house?

Self. There are always Uncles at Christmas. The same Uncles. And on Christmas mornings, with dog-disturbing whistle and sugar fags, I would scour the swathed town for the news of the little world, and find always a dead bird by the white Bank or by the deserted swings; perhaps a robin, all but one of his fires out, and that fire still burning on his breast. Men and women wading and scooping back from church or chapel, with taproom noses and wind-smacked cheeks, all albinos, huddled their stiff black jarring feathers against the irreligious snow. Mistletoe hung from the gas in all the front parlours; there was sherry and walnuts and bottled beer and crackers by the dessertspoons; and cats in their fur-abouts watched the fires; and the high-heaped fires crackled and spat, all ready for the chestnuts and the mulling pokers. Some few large men sat in the front parlours, without their collars, Uncles almost certainly, trying their new cigars, holding them out judiciously at arm's-length, returning them to their mouths, coughing, then

And, last of all, in the toe of the stocking, sixpence like a silver corn.

I would sit in the front room, among festoons and Chinese lanterns, and nibble at dates, and try to make a model man-o'-war . . .

holding them out again as though waiting for the explosion; and some few small aunts, not wanted in the kitchen, nor anywhere else for that matter, sat on the very edges of their chairs, poised and brittle, afraid to break, like faded cups and saucers. Not many those mornings trod the piling streets: an old man always, fawn-bowlered, yellow-gloved, and, at this time of year, with spats of snow, would take his constitutional to the white bowling-green, and back, as he would take it wet or fine on Christmas Day or Doomsday; sometimes two hale young men, with big pipes blazing, no overcoats, and windblown scarves, would trudge, unspeaking, down to the forlorn sea, to work up an appetite, to blow away the fumes, who knows, to walk into the waves until nothing of them was left but the two curling smoke clouds of their inextinguishable briars.

Small Boy. Why didn't you go home for Christmas dinner?

Self. Oh, but I did, I always did. I would be slap-dashing home, the gravy smell of the dinners of others, the bird smell, the brandy, the pudding and mince, weaving up my nostrils, when out of a snow-clogged side-lane would come a boy the spit of myself, with a pink-tipped cigarette and the violet past of a black eye, cocky as a bullfinch, leering all to himself. I hated him on sight and sound, and would be about to put my dog-whistle to my lips and blow him off the face of Christmas when suddenly he, with a violet wink, put *his* whistle to *his* lips and blew so stridently, so high, so exquisitely loud, that gobbling faces, their cheeks bulged with goose, would press against their tinselled windows, the whole length of the white echoing street.

Small Boy. What did you have for dinner?

Self. Turkey, and blazing pudding.

Small Boy. Was it nice?

Self. It was not made on earth.

Small Boy. What did you do after dinner?

Self. The Uncles sat in front of the fire, took off their collars, loosened all buttons, put their large moist hands over their watch-chains, groaned a little, and slept. Mothers, aunts, and sisters scuttled to and fro, bearing tureens. The dog was sick. Auntie Beattie had to have three aspirins, but Auntie Hannah, who liked port, stood in the middle of the snowbound back-yard, singing like a big-bosomed thrush. I would blow up balloons to see how big they would blow up to; and, when they burst, which they all did, the Uncles jumped and rumbled. In the rich and heavy afternoon, the Uncles breathing like dolphins and the snow descending, I would sit in the front room, among festoons and Chinese lanterns, and nibble at dates, and try to make a model man-o'-war, following the Instructions for Little Engineers, and produce what might be mistaken for a sea-going tram. And then, at Christmas tea, the recovered Uncles would be jolly over their mince-pies; and the great iced cake loomed in the centre of the table like a marble grave. Auntie Hannah laced her tea with rum, because it was only once a year. And in the evening, there was Music. An uncle played the fiddle, a cousin sang "Cherry Ripe," and another uncle sang "Drake's Drum." It was very warm in the little house. Auntie Hannah, who had got on to the parsnip wine, sang a song about Rejected Love, and Bleeding Hearts, and Death, and then another in which she said that her Heart was like a Bird's Nest; and then everybody laughed again, and then I went to bed. Looking through my bedroom window, out into the moonlight and the flying, unending, smoke-coloured snow, I could see the lights in the windows of all the other houses on our hill, and hear the music rising from them up the long, steadily falling night. I turned the gas down, I got into bed. I said some words to the close and holy darkness, and then I slept.

Small Boy. But it all sounds like an ordinary Christmas.

Self. It was.

Small Boy. But Christmas when you were a boy wasn't any different to Christmas now.

Self. It was, it was.

Small Boy. Why was Christmas different then?

Self. I mustn't tell you.

Small Boy. Why mustn't you tell me? Why is Christmas different for me?

Self. I mustn't tell you.

Small Boy. Why can't Christmas be the same for me as it was for you when you were a boy?

Self. I mustn't tell you. I mustn't tell you because it is Christmas now.

Christmas Bells

I heard the bells on Christmas Day
Their old, familiar carols play,
And wild and sweet
The words repeat
Of peace on earth, good-will to men!

And thought how, as the day had come,
The belfries of all Christendom
Had rolled along
The unbroken song
Of peace on earth, good-will to men!

Till, ringing, swinging on its way,
The world revolved from night to day,
A voice, a chime,
A chant sublime
Of peace on earth, good-will to men!

Then from each black, accursed mouth
The cannon thundered in the South,
And with the sound
The carols drowned
Of peace on earth, good-will to men!

It was as if an earthquake rent
The hearth-stones of a continent,
And made forlorn
The households born
Of peace on earth, good-will to men!

And in despair I bowed my head;
"There is no peace on earth," I said;
"For hate is strong,
And mocks the song
Of peace on earth, good-will to men!"

Then pealed the bells more loud and deep:
"God is not dead; nor doth He sleep!
The Wrong shall fail,
The Right prevail,
With peace on earth, good-will to men!"

Henry Wadsworth Longfellow (1807-1882)

Longfellow wrote this poem on Christmas Day 1864. The fourth and fifth stanzas refer to the U.S. Civil War, then nearing its end. The poem inspired "I Heard the Bells on Christmas Day," the carol written by John Baptiste Calkin in 1872.

CHRISTMAS, 1863.

A Christmas Alphabet

by Marion Conger

A is for Angels, Appearing on high, proclaiming glad news from a clear midnight sky. **B** is Balthazar, Black King from afar, who journeyed to Bethlehem led by a star, Bearing gifts to the **C**hild born that first Christmas day and laid in a Cradle on Cushions of hay. **D**'s for the Dolls of which little girls Dream, **E** for an Eggnog with nutmeg and cream. **F** is a Fir tree made Festive and bright by candles a Family has gathered to light, by silvery **G**arlands and Gewgaws of Gold, and all that its fragrant Green branches can hold of Gingerbread babies and cranberry strings and other most Gorgeously Glittering things. **H** is for Holly wreaths decking the Halls, and Hemlock boughs Hung on the living-room walls. **I** is for Ice skaters racing together, on Indigo ponds in Icicle weather. **J** is the Jewel-colored Jellies and Jams served with turkeys and geese and with clove-studded hams. **K** is Kris Kringle, whose cheeks are like cherries, and the magical Knapsack of Khaki he carries, full of Kites and Kaleidoscopes, Kerchiefs and Kittens, and stuffed Kangaroos and gay Knitted mittens. **L** is for Logs that are Laid on the hearth to burn when the winter sweeps out of the north.

M is for Misty-eyed Maidens and Misses who stand 'neath the Mistletoe waiting for kisses. N is for Nuts with a Nutcracker handy. O is for Oranges and Oodles of candy. P is Plum Puddings with hard sauce on top, and Pies made of Pumpkin, and Popcorn to Pop. Q is a warm patchwork Quilt on a bed. R is for Ribbons of Raspberry Red. S is for Sleighs and for Sleds and for Skis, Skimming over the Snow with the greatest of ease. T is for Tops, and for all of the Toys, like Trumpets and Tom-toms, that make a fine noise. U is a Useful, Uninteresting box of Umbrellas and Underwear, mufflers and socks. V is a Vigorous reindeer named Vixen who, with Dancer and Prancer and Donder and Blitzen, flies around the World like the down of a thistle When Saint Nick cracks his Whip and gives them a Whistle. X is for Xmas cards come by the dozens from aunts and from uncles, from friends and from cousins. Y is a Yule candle lighted each Year, and the Yawning of Youngsters as bedtime draws near. Z is a Zebra with shoe-button eyes, peeking out of a stocking in happy surprise, and looking as if—if he could— he would say, "Merry Christmas to all, and to all a good day!"

My Father's Perfect Christmas

by THOMAS CAHILL

I CANNOT TRIM the Christmas tree without thinking of my father, who always had a method. For him there was a right way and a wrong way to do everything.

There were things he didn't do well—such as sing—and things he didn't do at all—such as draw. Those things—the artistic things—he left to "your mother's side" and to the strain from my mother's side that showed up one way or another in most of his six children. The artistic things seemed to puzzle him and leave him mute. He just didn't get it.

He and his four brothers (he was the baby of the line) were practical guys who got things done. Like many practical people, they had little to say. My mother and her sisters could talk for hours about God-knew-what, but my father and his brothers seldom communicated to one another or to anyone else.

It wasn't their maleness that made them taciturn, I knew that. Their mother, my grandmother, never had anything to say either. Once, at a birthday party for one of my sisters, the flames atop the birthday candles spread to the paper tablecloth. Grandma, silent as ever, her stout frame swaddled in perpetual black, rose from her chair with the speed of an Olympic runner and swatted those flames with her brick-heavy black pocketbook. Bam, bam! My mother returned from the kitchen to find the cake smashed and a dozen little girls in tears.

"There was a fire, Margaret," said Grandma, who looked very much like George Washington, once more resuming her seat and her Mount Rushmore silence. Practical. Not especially graceful. But practical.

My father, the gentlest of the bunch of brothers, was the only one who could be called a gentleman. He was tough, all right, and like his brothers made for anything. But he dressed more gravely, moved more smoothly, talked more sonorously than they.

He even had a playful side, though it was one he displayed only within the confines of his family. There were nights—few and far between, I'm afraid—when he would dress up as a character named Gertie

Gitchiedrawers and entertain us, hilarious in our beds, with an apron at his waist and a dish towel around his head. Gertie Gitchiedrawers was both fastidious and overbearing, rigid and sentimental—the sort of old-maid baby-sitter every child dreads. She had a lot in common, I suspect, with women he did not like—a nun from long ago, old biddy contemporaries of his mother's, a sister-in-law or two. Gertie's *pièce de résistance* (which we all resisted with squirms and shrieks) was the implantation of a very wet, effusive kiss on the cheek of each child.

Every once in a great while he would take us to a first-run movie, which involved a cab ride from our Bronx apartment into Manhattan. (Cabbies and other working men were always properly addressed as "Chief.") There were so many of us for my mother to feed and clothe beforehand that we invariably arrived after a long line had formed.

"Oh, Dad," we would say, "we'll never get in this time." But Dad would turn his chiseled face to some especially vulnerable lady near the front of the line, wink at her and hold up so many fingers—four or five or however many tickets he needed. Inevitably, the chosen lady would buy the tickets for him, trot over to exchange them for his cash and receive his most gracious smile and hat-tipping ceremony. She always looked pleased.

To a casual observer these might have seemed spontaneous demonstrations of Irish charm, but to my father they were conscious strategies—and he would always be happy to explain his methodology for picking out the right lady on the line.

He had a method for attending baseball games and another for viewing the St. Patrick's Day parade. He had a method for riding a bike—a good one, which he taught me, even though he himself had never ridden a bike. He had a method for playing golf, a method for making pancakes, a method for tossing salad, a method for carving turkey, a method for keeping a checkbook—one my mother could never catch on to no matter how many times he explained it to her.

. . .my father picked up the top half—now a perfect little tree—wished the couple a merry Christmas and took off.

We children noticed that it was not just we who called on him for help. Whenever adults got in impossible jams, my father became their Emergency Weapon. He was always helping more introverted, hysterical relatives in and out of cars, hospitals, mental institutions, funeral parlors and tax offices.

My favorite story of my father is the one he told me about the Christmas of 1940, my first Christmas. He had had to work till Christmas Eve night, returning home with his well-earned bonus and picking up a Christmas tree along the way. When he reached the tree lot, however, there was only one left. A large, imperious lady had already entered into negotiations for it.

She didn't care to pay full price because she didn't really want such a large tree. Dad promptly inserted himself into the haggle, offering to pay half and then divide the tree with the lady. Perfect, said she, provided only she should have the fuller half.

Together they purchased the tree, which my father lugged to her garage. There, her husband sawed it in half. The moment the trunk snapped in two, my father picked up the top half—now a perfect little tree—wished the couple a merry Christmas and took off. As he turned the corner, he glanced back to see the two just beginning to appreciate the strange, pointless bush the woman had so greedily insisted on.

Mary, my second sister and my parents' fourth child, was born in 1948 on December 23. Since there was no chance my mother would be home for Christmas Eve, I was called upon to stand in for her when, after the children were put to bed, the tree was decorated and the presents set forth.

Before she left for the hospital, my mother counseled me to be grown-up and helpful in my new role, but I, nearly nine, had no need of anyone's encouragement. The adulthood to be conferred by staying up was a pleasure beyond the reach of ordinary mortals.

What I remember of that night is not the presents we laid out for my brother and sister, sleeping unawares in a bedroom down the hall. Nor can I remember what St. Nicholas left for me to rediscover in the morning. What I remember is the quiet and the joy of working through the hours of darkness with my father.

The great task was the trimming of the tree—and of course he had a method. First, the electric bulbs, which had to be set well within the branches, so that their cords would not show and their lights would not be bald but refracted and mysterious. Next, the ornaments; and last, the tinsel icicles, which had to be hung strand by strand, not flung vulgarly in clumps as impatient, tasteless fathers did. Gradually, as we labored together, the tree assumed its annual splendor, which would awe my siblings on the morrow.

Many years later I learned that my father had never had a Christmas tree in his own childhood. His parents were immigrants, and his father died in a road construction accident when my father, baby Patrick, was but a few weeks old. My silent grandmother took in washing, often faced eviction and one day, in desperation, even placed my father's older brothers in an orphanage. But she returned to take them back the same day, and from that time they somehow squeaked by.

My father, who became quite deaf after a serious childhood illness, was taken to be a dunce by his teachers. He was saved from academic extinction by a kindly, perceptive nun who tutored him for a high school scholarship, a course that would eventually make him his family's only college graduate. But he struggled against the deafness all his life.

He once told me, during a crisis in my life, that all he had ever wanted to be was a father. I don't know, but perhaps that keen desire marshaled his abilities, as a magnet marshals iron filings, so that he was able to accomplish tasks he had no models and no preparation for.

Many years later I learned that my father had never had a Christmas tree in his own childhood.

At any rate, that Christmas of the tree-trimming was nearly 50 years ago, and this past summer my father was taken from us. For many years I trimmed a tree for my own children and, more recently, instructed them in the art. As I look back, my father's method seems true art, beginning in ritual and devotion and ending in a great symbol, set in our midst, of our mysterious relation to one another—father to son, brother to sister, husband to wife, friend to friend, generation upon generation. To me the annual rite is a kind of token of the splendor and the painful beauty of the universe itself.

Christmas Crafts

CREATE DAZZLING DECORATIONS AND STUNNING GIFTS
WITH STEP-BY-STEP SIMPLICITY

Decorations for Christmas

*The holiday season provides lots of opportunity to create decorations for the home.
Try a novel Advent Calendar, make a wreath you can use year after year—or even personalize
the holiday party favors that might adorn your dinner table on Christmas Day.*

Advent Calendar

This beautiful wall hanging can be used year after year. Children will enjoy putting the decorations in place each day. At the end of the season, the calendar can be rolled up for storage.

WHAT YOU NEED

+ 1 1/4 yards 72-inch-wide cream felt
+ cream thread
+ 6-strand embroidery floss to match cream, green, brown, and red felt, and all small felt squares
+ crewel needle
+ tracing paper
+ 12 x 36-inch rectangle green felt
+ 4-inch square brown felt
+ 5-inch square red felt
+ 3-inch felt squares in a variety of colors for decorations
+ variety of glass beads, sequins, gold cord, and ribbons to trim decorations
+ white craft glue
+ 24 small gold safety pins
+ two 11 1/2-inch lengths of 1/2-inch wooden doweling
+ 1 yard of thin silk cord

Preparing the felt

1 Cut two 40 x 25-inch pieces cream felt to form the background. From the remaining cream felt, cut two 24 x 2 3/4-inch pieces for the doweling pockets.
2 Center the pocket pieces across the top and bottom edges of one background piece, 1 inch inside the edges. Using cream thread, machine-stitch the pockets to the background, leaving the ends open. Put this piece aside.

Preparing the tree

1 Trace the tree pattern on page 32 and enlarge on a photocopier until the measurement from the base of

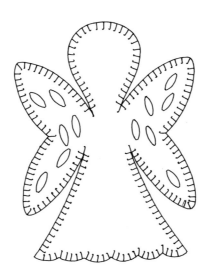

the pot to the top of the tree is 21 inches. Pin patterns to the green felt and cut out the tree.
2 Cut out the tree trunk in brown felt and the tree stand in red felt.
3 Position the felt shapes on the remaining background piece, with the top of the tree 5 1/2 inches down from the top edge, and the bottom of the tree stand about 3 1/2 inches from the bottom edge. Pin in place, with the pieces tightly butted.
4 Using two strands of matching floss, sew each shape to the background with blanket stitch (see page 34 for stitches used in this project).

Making the decorations

1 Trace the decoration patterns (above and on page 32). For each decoration, cut two identical pieces from colored felt—50 pieces in all.
2 Decorate the front of each shape as desired, using glue to attach the trimmings.
3 Join the front and back of each pair with the blanket stitch, using two strands of matching embroidery floss.

4 Take a small safety pin and hand-tack the side with the catch head to the back of the decoration.
5 Trace the outlines of all the decorations onto tracing paper. Pin to the tree, then, using two strands of yellow embroidery floss, work the outlines in running stitch. These indicate the positions for each decoration.

Finishing the calendar

1 Pin the two cream background pieces together, with the tree to the front and the doweling pockets to the back. Using two strands of matching embroidery floss and the blanket stitch, sew the two pieces together around the four sides.
2 Insert the doweling pieces in the pockets and glue the silk cord to the ends to hang up the calendar.
3 Place the decorations along the sides of the background. Beginning December 1, place one decoration on the tree each night until, on Christmas Eve, the tree is complete.

Trimming the Calendar

Decorate the tree with gold cord for sparkle.

For a quick alternative, mimic the embroidery stitches in the ornaments with tube puff paints (available at crafts and art-supply stores) in a variety of colors. Sequins and rhinestones can be pushed into the wet paint with tweezers to add sparkle. Use craft glue to attach the second felt layer to the back of the decorated layer.

The doweling can be painted to match your wall, extended beyond the width of the calendar, and decorated with fancy tassels or cords.

The personal touch for the holidays includes an Advent Calendar
for the children, a Christmas wreath to welcome family and friends, and
a box of holiday party favors to add some fun to the festivities.

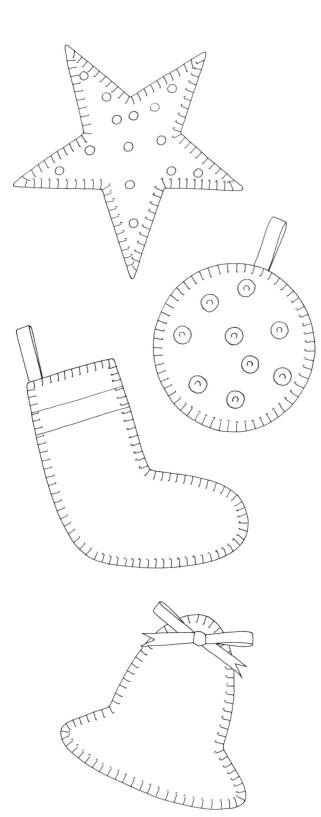

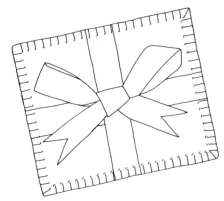

Trace the patterns above and then enlarge them on a photo-copier by 20 percent. Trace and enlarge the tree pattern until the measurement from the base of the pot to the top of the tree is 21 inches. Use these patterns on cards, tags, and other items.

Holiday Party Favors

Create colorful Christmas crackers and crepe-paper hats for your own or your host's table. Fill the crackers with small novelty items. To make a special box for these favors, see the instructions below.

WHAT YOU NEED

- ✦ Crepe paper, for hats
- ✦ ruler
- ✦ sharp scissors, pinking shears
- ✦ regular and double-sided transparent tape
- ✦ star stickers
- ✦ 8 paper-towel or other cardboard tubes cut into 5-inch lengths
- ✦ 3 to 4 sheets gift wrap
- ✦ ribbon or cord, about 3 yards
- ✦ gifts for inside favors
- ✦ seals, tassels, colored pens
- ✦ tissue paper in two colors
- ✦ box to hold favors

Making the hats

1 Cut six pieces of crepe paper 24 x 6 inches. Make six party hats, following the directions on page 34.

Making the crackers

1 In each piece of cardboard tubing, insert a gift, surprises, and rolled-up hat.

2 Cut six pieces of wrapping paper

A box of holiday party favors makes a fun gift for a host or hostess. For your own table, make enough for all your guests. Choose colors to match your linen and china, or use the most colorful paper you can find. You might also write out riddles, fortunes, or humorous messages to include among the gifts.

into 15 x 7-inch rectangles. Use pinking shears to trim the short edges. Center a favor-filled tube at the long edge of a piece of gift wrap. Secure the paper to the tube with regular transparent tape. Roll the paper tightly around the tube and secure the seam invisibly with

double-sided transparent tape.

3 Carefully tie a 9-inch piece of ribbon or cord around the favor wrappings on both ends of the tube, drawing in the paper evenly.

4 Repeat to make the other favors, then decorate as you wish with tassels, seals, stickers, or ribbons.

MAKING THE BOX FOR THE FAVORS

1 Lay two layers of tissue paper flat on a smooth work surface. Center the gift box on top of the tissue paper. Using a pencil, draw the outline of the bottom of the box on the tissue paper. Gently remove the box.

2 Measure the height of the box, add 2 inches to that number, then add the measurement to all 4 sides of the box outline. (If, for example, the box is 2 inches tall, put marks at intervals 4 inches outside the original outline.)

3 Draw the new, larger rectangle around the original one. With scissors, cut out a square at each corner, using the inner rectangle as the inside guide. Cutting away this excess will allow the tissue to fit the box corners neatly.

4 Using the scissors, cut the 2-inch edge of the tissue in a zigzag pattern. Then place the tissue in the box, matching the outline to the inside bottom of the box. Place gifts in the box and fold the zigzag edge decoratively over the edge.

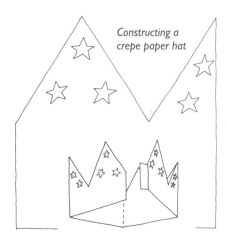

Constructing a crepe paper hat

Fold the crepe paper in half crosswise, twice. Cut to the shape above. Unfold, then join the ends with regular transparent tape on the inside, overlapping the ends slightly. Decorate with star stickers. Fold up the bottom of the hat 2 inches, so that it will fit inside the tube when it is rolled up. Insert the rolled hat in the tube.

Stitching Techniques

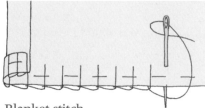

Blanket stitch

Baste hem in fabric. Bring the thread out below edge of hem. Insert a needle from the right, bringing it down below hem. With thread from the previous stitch under the needle point, draw the needle through to form a stitch over the edge.

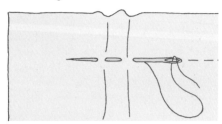

Running stitch

Weave the point of the needle in and out of the fabric several times before pulling the needle through. Keep the stitches and the spaces between them small and even. Unlike basting, this stitch is usually meant to be permanent.

Fresh pine foliage—with its crisp, evergreen aroma—is used to great effect in this version of the Christmas wreath described above right.

Christmas Wreath

Celebrate Christmas elegantly with this colorful wreath. Hung on the front door or an inside wall, it will be a cheery sight all through the festive season. If you choose to use artificial greenery, your wreath will last a lifetime.

WHAT YOU NEED

✦ Four 20-inch lengths of ribbon, in widths and colors of your choice
✦ wreath base made from twisted vines
✦ real or artificial pine boughs or holly
✦ artificial fruit
✦ hot glue gun

1 Tie the ribbons into four bows.
2 Arrange greenery, fruit, and ribbons on the wreath base, trying various placements.
3 When you are happy with the arrangement, cut the pine boughs to the desired length. Using the hot-glue gun, glue the cut ends of the pine to the wreath base.

4 Repeat with fruit and finish off with bows.
5 There is no need to add a loop for hanging, since a vine wreath is easily hung on a nail or hook. Hang the wreath on a door or wall, making sure the nail or hook is not visible.

Making Holly Wreaths

For a traditional Christmas wreath, substitute fresh holly boughs for the needled greenery. Cut a few small, healthy branches. Submerge the ends in water until you are ready to assemble the wreath. Strip small clumps of leaves from the branches and trim the ends, leaving a little of the twig to poke into the wreath base. Attach the holly in the same way as the pine wreath. Small clumps are easier to work with than big bundles. Decorate with fruit and ribbon or in any way you wish.

Cards, Wraps, Tags and Boxes

GREETING CARDS
Make lovely Christmas cards from magazine art, fabric, colored paper.

Magazine-Weave Card
The impact of this type of card comes from the blend of tones—it's like a woven carpet.

WHAT YOU NEED
+ 6 x 10-inch card stock colored paper
+ glue stick
+ colorful magazine images
+ craft knife
+ grid ruler
+ cardboard
+ dressmaker's pins

Preparing the cardboard
1 On the card stock, score a center line from one long side to the other. Fold in half, creating a 5 x 6-inch card.
2 Cut two pieces of colored paper 4 3/4 x 5 3/4 inches. Apply glue to the back of one piece; center and glue it to the card front.

Weaving and gluing
1 Using the knife and ruler, cut eight strips 1/2 x 5 inches from the magazine images. Arrange them, long edges together and desired image face down on the cardboard. Stab a pin in the end of each strip.
2 Cut 10 strips 1/2 x 5 inches. Hold one strip in a horizontal position and weave it under and over the pinned strips; push it against the top pins. Weave the next strip over and under and push it against the first woven strip. Weave all the strips in this alternating arrangement.
3 Apply the glue stick to the second piece of colored paper and press it to the back of the woven strips. Remove the pins from the strips.
4 Turn the weaving right side up. Use the knife and ruler to trim away the unwoven ends. Glue the weaving to the card front, centering it on the colored paper.

Fabric-Covered Card
Use motifs from fabric to create an appealing floral montage.

WHAT YOU NEED
+ thick cardboard
+ fabric and colored paper
+ length of ribbon
+ craft knife
+ ruler
+ scissors
+ white craft glue
+ hole punch or awl

Preparing the cardboard
1 Using the craft knife, cut out two 5 x 7 1/2-inch pieces of cardboard.
2 On one piece draw a 3-inch-square window 1 1/2 inches from the top and 1 inch in from each side. Using the knife and ruler, cut out the window.

Gluing and cutting the fabric
1 With the scissors, cut a 7 x 9-inch piece of fabric. Apply glue to one side of the cardboard with the window. Center and glue the cardboard to the wrong side of the fabric.
2 Trim the fabric diagonally at the corners. Fold the fabric borders over the edges of the cardboard and glue them down.
3 From corner to corner, cut an X in the fabric covering the window. Wrap the fabric triangles over the edges of the window, trim as necessary, and glue to the back of the cardboard.
4 Cut a 4 3/4 x 7 1/4-inch piece of fabric. Apply glue to the back of the cardboard with the window, ensuring that it is coated to the edges. Center the wrong side of the fabric over the cardboard. Press firmly and allow to dry.
5 Turn the cardboard window side up. Use the knife to cut a hole in the backing fabric, along the edges of the window.
6 Cover the second piece of cardboard with the colored paper, front and back.

7 Determine the center point on the left long side of both pieces of cardboard. Punch a hole on either side of the center point on each piece, 1/2 inch in from the edge.
8 Thread the ribbon through the holes and secure the bow. Do not make the bow too tight.
9 Center a picture, photograph, cutout, greeting, or sticker in the window and write your message inside the card beneath it.

GIFT WRAPS
Take any plain paper and dress it up to make imaginative Christmas wrapping.

Potato-Print Wrap
Get the children to help make wrapping paper using this easy, effective method.

WHAT YOU NEED
+ sheet of tracing paper
+ potato
+ craft knife
+ sheets of paper appropriate for wrapping paper
+ artist's acrylic paints
+ artist's paintbrush

Preparing the stencil
1 Trace the outline of the star stencil pattern (see page 41). Choose a potato that, when cut in half, is large enough to accommodate the motif. Place the tracing on top of the cut side of the potato. With the craft knife, cut along each line of the star to a depth of about 1/2 inch. Turn the potato on its side and cut away the area outside the star by slicing horizontally 1/2 inch deep between the star points.

Stamping the motif
1 Lay the sheets of paper on a flat surface. Using the paintbrush, dab paint on the potato star to cover.
2 Stamp the motif on the paper; then, holding the paper with one hand, lift the potato off. Repeat until the sheet is covered. Let the paper dry.

A great variety of paper and fabric gift wraps, cards, and tags can be made using the projects on these pages as a start. Make them as simple or as elaborate as you like, from an attractive Christmas card to a stunning gift wrap for a special friend: **1** Potato-print wrap, **2** Stenciled tag and card, **3** Variety tags and cards, **4** Ribbon Christmas tree, **5** Corrugated wrap.

Scribble Wrap

Making candle scribble paper is quite easy and quick. Vary wax applications for different effects.

WHAT YOU NEED

- sheets of paper (the paper will be wet with a sponge, so it cannot be too thin)
- white candle
- artist's acrylic paint
- sponge

How to scribble wax

1 This technique can be quite messy, so spread plenty of newspaper on your work surface before you start. Lay the sheets of paper to be colored on top.

2 Take the candle and scribble wax all over the paper until the paper is well covered.

Painting the wrapping

1 Dilute the paint with water to a watery consistency: You will need enough to cover all the sheets you intend to color. Dip the sponge in the paint and draw it over the paper to cover the sheet completely. Allow each sheet to dry.

2 For a deeper color, you will need about three layers of paint. Allow the paper to dry between each coat. Alternatively, for a more subtle effect, you can add more wax scribbles over the first layer of paint and each subsequent layer. Allow each layer to dry.

Spatter Wrap

Use richly colored paper and gold or silver paint to impart a seasonal richness with this technique.

WHAT YOU NEED

- colored sheets of paper appropriate for wrapping
- acrylic paint
- large brush

1 This technique can be messy, so spread plenty of newspaper on your work surface. Lay the sheets of paper to be spattered on top.

2 Wet the brush with plenty of paint and, with a flicking action, spatter the wrapping sheet. The size of spatters and coverage of the paper will depend on the size of brush, the viscosity of the paint, and the flicking technique. It is a good idea to experiment with scrap paper until you have a result you are happy with.

3 Allow the paper to dry.

Corrugated Wrap

The texture of corrugated paper gives dimension to a gift wrap. Even the smallest gift can look special. It is best if the present is a rectangular shape, such as a book, but with a little imagination, most objects can be wrapped this way.

WHAT YOU NEED

- sheet of colored paper
- sheet of thin, colored corrugated cardboard (or color it with acrylic paint)
- sheet of tracing paper
- craft knife
- awl
- ribbon and 5 inches of cord

Preparing the cardboard

1 Wrap a gift with the colored paper. Place the wrapped gift on the corrugated cardboard and cut a piece large enough to wrap around it.

2 On the piece of tracing paper, trace the star stencil pattern on page 41, and lay the tracing on the cardboard in the position you want the cutout to appear. Using the knife, carefully cut out a star. Repeat so that you have two corrugated star cutouts to decorate the top.

3 Wrap the corrugated cardboard around the present; tie and knot the ribbon to hold the edges of the corrugated cardboard in place.

Preparing the stars

1 With the awl, pierce a hole through the center of both corrugated stars.

2 Thread the cord through one and tie a knot in the end. Thread the other end of the cord through the other star and knot. Push both stars against the knots.

3 Attach the center of the cord to the knot of ribbon.

INNOVATIVE GIFT WRAPS

With these novel ideas, the wrapping becomes part of the gift. Give a little thought to coordinating the wrap and gift—for example, choose a wine-colored napkin to wrap a bottle of red wine.

Kitchen Gift Wrap

Choose a colorful kitchen towel for this practical wrapping.

WHAT YOU NEED

- new kitchen towel
- sewing needle
- thread to match kitchen towel
- rope, enough to go around package twice and leave 2 1/2 inches at each end
- 2 cookie cutters
- 2 wooden cooking spoons

1 Wrap the item with the kitchen towel as you would with a sheet of paper. Fold over the ends neatly and tack them with the needle and thread—don't stitch too securely.
2 Make a knot at each end of the rope. Tie the package with the rope, looping the cookie cutters and spoons into the final tie. For a homespun touch, make a knot instead of a bow.

Japanese Gift Wrap

Choose filmy fabric or scarves for this project. Fabrics of different textures and thicknesses will add interest to your wrap.

WHAT YOU NEED

- 2 squares fabric or 2 scarves
- needle and thread, or sewing machine

1 Hem all edges of the fabric by hand or machine (not necessary if using scarves).
2 Lay one piece of fabric on top of the other and place the item to be wrapped on a diagonal in the center of the fabric. Bring two opposite corners of the fabric together and fold neatly over each other. Bring the other opposite corners together and tie. Tuck in all the edges to make a neat parcel.

Book Gift Wrap

For a special book, create a wrapping that will later act as a decorative and protective envelope. A book for a gardener can be wrapped in a floral print; a country-style cookbook, in gingham.

WHAT YOU NEED

- rectangular piece of fabric, for pocket
- contrasting fabric, for flap
- fabric scissors
- needle and thread, or sewing machine
- 2 buttons, about 1-inch diameter
- silk cord, about 12 inches

Preparing the fabric

1 Measure the height, width, and thickness of the book. Cut a rectangle of fabric. The length should double the book's height plus the thickness plus 1/2-inch seam allowance on each side. The width should be the book's width plus the thickness plus 1 inch. One of the rectangle's short ends should be on the selvage.
2 Cut a square of contrasting fabric to equal the width of the rectangle. With right sides facing, stitch one side of the square to the nonselvage end of the rectangle. Press. Turn under a 1/2-inch hem on the opposite side of the square. Press.
3 Fold each end of the combined strip in to meet at the join, right sides facing (below). Pin, then stitch each side, 1/2 inch from each edge.
4 Turn the pocket and flap right side out. Slipstitch the pressed hem to close the open end of the flap.

Finishing touches

1 Slip the book into the bag and mark the position of the two buttons,

one on the flap and one on the pocket, centered. Sew on the buttons. Tie one end of the cord around the thread of the flap button and tie a knot in the other end of the cord.
2 With the book inside the bag, wind the cord around the buttons in a figure 8 pattern to secure the parcel.

Flower Pot Gift Wrap

This is a quick and attractive way to dress up a potted plant.

WHAT YOU NEED

- 2 large new bandannas or colorful square napkins
- cloth tape

1 Fold one bandanna diagonally in half and tie it around the rim of the pot with a simple knot (the folded edge runs around the rim and the loose points of the handkerchief hang down). Tuck the pointed end of the triangle under the pot and tape it in place.
2 Repeat with the other handkerchief, tying the knot on the opposite side of the rim.

Baby Gift Wrap

The wrapping on this baby gift may prove as useful as the present itself.

WHAT YOU NEED

- cloth diaper
- 3 diaper pins
- small teddy bear for trim
- ribbon for bow

1 Lay the diaper flat on a table with a corner toward you. Place the gift item (a square or rectangular

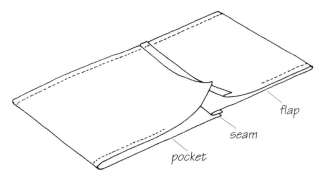

flap

seam

pocket

The extra thought that has been given to the wrapping of these gifts has added greatly to their charm. Clockwise from the left: Bottle Gift Wrap; Japanese Gift Wrap; Kitchen Gift Wrap; and Book Gift Wrap.

shape is best) in the center of the diaper, at a 45-degree angle to the sides. (For a gift that is too large to be accommodated this way, use a baby's bath towel.)

2 Fold the top corner of the diaper down over the gift, then fold in the two side corners. Finally, fold up the bottom corner to overlap the other corners. Pin the four corners together with two diaper pins, making sure you don't damage the item inside.

3 Tie a ribbon bow around the teddy bear's neck. Thread the ribbon

through the hole at the end of the remaining diaper pin and attach the teddy bear to the gift.

Bottle Gift Wrap

Turn a bottle of wine or sparkling cider— or a bottle of flavored oil or vinegar—into an elegant gift with this easy gift wrap.

WHAT YOU NEED

✦ colorful cloth napkin
✦ cloth tape in matching color
✦ contrasting ribbon, for bow

1 Lay the napkin on a table. Place the bottle on one edge of the napkin

with the bottom of the bottle about 1 1/2 inches from the bottom of the napkin. Secure the napkin to the bottle with cloth tape, about halfway down the bottle, and fold down the top edge of the napkin a little above the top of the bottle.

2 Roll up the bottle tightly in the napkin and secure the end of the napkin with tape.

3 Tuck the bottom of the napkin under the bottle and secure with tape. Tie a bow around the neck of the bottle.

GIFT TAGS

Use the wrapping paper for your gift as material for the tag, or adapt our Christmas card ideas to this use. Below are more suggestions.

Novelty Tags

Tags can be made from any number of found objects, photocopies, cutouts of fabric or colored paper, magazine pictures, tassels, ribbons—the key is your imagination.

WHAT YOU NEED

- card stock
- glue stick
- white craft glue
- ribbon or cord
- craft knife
- scissors
- ruler

1 Cut the card to a suitable shape. If the tag is to be shaped (a Christmas bell, for example, from the Advent Calendar on page 32), glue all the elements onto the card first, then cut out the shape.

2 Arrange colored paper, photocopies, magazine pictures, or found

Making the job easier

Make photocopied wrapping paper by copying on colored papers, or by adding color highlights with acrylic paints and a brush.

A hole punch is useful for punching holes in thin cardboard and paper, especially if you are making a large number of tags.

A dressmaker's awl or an ice pick is useful for piercing holes in thick cardboard and cardboard covered with fabric. Or you can use a nail and hammer. Place the nail tip at the hole position and hit the head until the nail protrudes through the card. Do this on some scrap wood or a few sheets of scrap cardboard so that you don't punch holes in your table or floor.

Ribbon is available at crafts stores as well as fabric stores. You can buy it by the yard or by the roll, which is usually less expensive.

---

objects on the card until you are happy with the result.

3 Glue the elements to the card, using the glue stick for paper and white craft glue for sequins, beads, or bulky items.

4 Punch a hole in the top or corner of the tag and attach the ribbon or cord for the tie (see the box on decorative ties, facing page).

Stenciled Tags

Stenciling is one of the quickest ways to make gift tags. You can buy stencils at crafts stores, or you can design and cut your own.

WHAT YOU NEED

- card stock, stencil
- artist's acrylic paint
- stencil brush
- ribbon or cord
- craft knife
- ruler

1 Cut the tags to the size and shape required and position the stencil on a card.

2 Wet the brush with a small

Make an assortment of gift tags in your spare time throughout the year so that when Christmas comes, you have a good supply to choose from.

amount of paint (to avoid bleeding around the edges of the motif, it's best if the brush is not saturated). Being careful not to wipe the paint under the stencil edges, dab the paint over the cutout until the area is covered. Holding the paper with one hand, carefully lift off the stencil and allow the tag to dry.

3 Punch a hole in the top or corner and attach the ribbon or cord for the tie.

Ribbon Christmas Tree

Vary the colors of this gift tag, perhaps blue and silver or green and gold, for a change from the standard green and red. Or coordinate the colors with your gift wrap.

WHAT YOU NEED

- Poster board in the colors of your choice
- craft knife
- ruler
- scissors

+ 1 1/3 yards 1/8-inch-wide ribbon for each tree
+ 12 inches 1/4-inch-wide ribbon for each tree
+ tapestry needle

Cutting the triangles

1 From the poster board, cut triangles 4 inches wide at the base and 5 inches high.

2 On a scrap of card, mark 11 intervals, 1/2 inch apart, along one edge. This will be the template for cutting the notches for the ribbon.

Using the template

1 Lay the template along one side of the triangle. Starting 1/2 inch from the base, snip a 1/8-inch notch at each mark on the template. Repeat on the other side.

2 Using the tapestry needle, make a small hole between the two notches at the top of the triangle.

Adding the ribbon

1 Fold the length of narrow ribbon in half to determine the center point. Place the center point midway between the first two notches at the base of the triangle and start crisscrossing the ribbon around the tree, pulling it into the notches and crossing each end over as if you were threading shoe laces. Pull the ribbon tightly into each notch as you go.

2 When you reach the last two notches at the top of the triangle, thread both ends of ribbon through the eye of the tapestry needle and push them through the hole.

Tying the bow

1 Fold the wider ribbon in half to determine the center point. Cross the two ends at the center point to form a loose bow. Pass the double strand of narrow ribbon from the top of the tree around the center of the bow and back through the hole. Pull the needle through until the bow is held tightly—this forms the "knot" of the bow and secures the bow to the card.

2 Remove the needle and tie the two ends in a knot behind the hole.

Trim the ends of the narrow ribbons about 6 inches above the top of the tag and knot them together to make a loop for hanging.

Paper Tassels

Use these tassels as napkin rings for the festive table, to coordinate with your gift wraps, or as an attractive trim for the tree.

WHAT YOU NEED

+ thick cardboard
+ craft knife
+ awl
+ sheet of white paper of the length you want your "cord"
+ white craft glue
+ artist's acrylic paints
+ brush

1 Cut out two cardboard tassel shapes and punch a hole in the top of each.

2 Roll and twist the white paper to look like a cord. (If you want cords that are longer than your paper, tape strips together and roll them with the tape on the inside.)

3 Thread one end of the cord through one of the tassels. Repeat

with the other tassel and the other end of cord. Glue the ends of the cord to the back of each tassel.

4 Cross the cord over until the tassels are sitting side by side. Glue the cord together at the point of crossing. When the glue is dry, paint the cord and cardboard with acrylic paint. Add black lines as shown in the photograph on the facing page to give the tassels definition.

Star Stencil Pattern

Use a photocopier to enlarge for required size.

Decorative Ties

Ties made from ribbon or cord can finish off a card or tag with flair. Ribbon comes in many colors, textures, and widths. When making a card with a specific theme and in specific colors, it's a good idea to take samples to the store so that you can choose a ribbon that suits. A few strands of raffia also make an effective tie for a parcel wrapped in something as simple as white butcher's paper or plain brown paper.

Attaching a bow to a gift tag

Method 1—one wide and one narrow ribbon
Fold the wide ribbon in half to determine the center point. Cross the two ends at this point to form a loose bow. Thread one end of the narrow ribbon through the hole in the tag from the back and pass it around the center of the loose bow. Thread the narrow ribbon back through the hole, pull it tight, and tie a knot. This will secure the bow to the tag.

Method 2—two equal ribbons
Punch two holes in the top of a tag, 1/2 inch

apart. Thread ribbons into the large eye of a needle. Insert the needle into the front of one hole and pull several inches to the back. Insert the needle into the second hole and bring the ribbons to the front. Remove the needle. Adjust the ribbons so that the ends are equal at the front of each hole. Tie a bow.

Attaching cord and ribbon ties

Tie the ends of a ribbon together in a firm knot. Pass the loop through the hole in the card or tag, pull it through a short way, and thread the knotted end through the loop. Let go of the loop and pull the knotted end firmly. Alternatively, simply pull a length of ribbon or cord through the hole and tie the ends together in a knot.

Finishing touch

Don't forget to finish off your ribbon ends, using sharp scissors to cut either a diagonal or a fishtail. This is not only a decorative element but also a practical one because it will minimize fraying at the end of the ribbon.

GIFT BOXES

Bright and imaginative presentation gives a thrill of pleasure even before the gift itself is revealed.

Wrapped and Painted

Gift boxes can be recycled from former gifts or bought inexpensively at card and crafts shops.

WHAT YOU NEED

Painted Box
- artist's acrylic paints
- paintbrush
- white craft glue

Fabric-covered Box
- fabric to cover
- white craft glue
- ribbon

Paper-covered Box
- paper to cover
- glue stick
- acrylic paint
- stencil
- stencil brush

Making a painted box

1 Paint the box in colors the recipient will like. You may need up to three coats of paint for even coverage.

2 When the paint is dry, you may wish to glue a cheerful figure to the top of the lid.

Making covered boxes

1 Cover each box with fabric or paper. To achieve the neatest finish, experiment with the corner folds before you glue them.

2 Decorate the paper-covered box with stencils and allow to dry. Glue ribbon to the lid of the fabric-covered box with craft glue. Pushpins are useful for holding the ribbon in place while the glue dries. Tie the ribbon bow and glue it to the top. For contrast, consider painting parts of the fabric on the lid with acrylic paint mixed with a little glue.

Reversing the fabric

1 As an alternative, when covering the lid, you might reverse the fabric if the wrong side provides a pleasing contrast.

Doric Column Box

This intriguing container may have the recipient puzzled for a few moments about how to open it — the bottom pulls out. Fill it with candy sticks, colored pencils, or rolled-up paper items.

WHAT YOU NEED

- corrugated cardboard
- thick cardboard
- craft knife
- ruler
- pencil
- gold acrylic paint
- white craft glue
- brush
- 2 small paper clips
- hair dryer (optional)

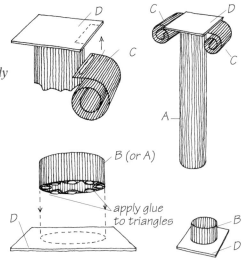

apply glue to triangles

Cutting the cardboard

1 Cut out the corrugated cardboard as shown below (note the direction of the corrugations): one piece A, $7^1/2$ x $12^1/2$ inches; one piece B, $7^1/2$ x $13^3/4$ inches; two pieces C, $2^1/8$ x $5^1/2$ inches. Cut out two pieces of the thick cardboard $2^3/4$ inches square (D). Paint one side of pieces A and B, and both sides of pieces C and D with gold paint and allow to dry.

2 On pieces A and B, mark a line $3/8$ inch from one end. Score this line with the blunt side of the craft knife on the corrugated side. Clip out triangle shapes along the scored border, leaving the last $3/4$ inch clear for overlap.

Making the cylinders

1 Apply glue on one long edge of piece A and fit the two edges together with a $3/4$-inch overlap, to form a tube. Hold in place with paper clips while glue dries—use a hair dryer to speed up the process. Repeat with piece B, with an overlap of a little more than $3/4$ inch, so that the tube it makes fits inside the tube formed by A.

2 On each cylinder, bend triangles inward, apply glue to them, and press each cylinder onto the center of piece D. Allow to dry.

3 Take two pieces C and curl into a spiral by rolling them tightly and then releasing the spiral. When you are satisfied with the spiral, apply glue to the top of the edge and attach to the column, as shown above. Hold firmly with clips while drying with a hair dryer.

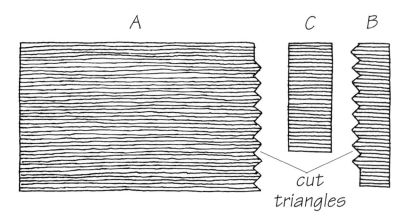

cut triangles

Simple Box

You can make this perfect cube any size you wish.

WHAT YOU NEED

+ cardboard
+ craft knife
+ ruler and pencil
+ white craft glue

Preparing the box

1 Decorate one side of a piece of cardboard with potato prints or stencils or cover with some attractive paper. The side you have decorated will be called the "right side."

2 Using the template (see below), mark the dimensions you require on the wrong side of the cardboard with a pencil and ruler.

3 Using the craft knife and ruler, cut around the outside edges. Score the fold lines on the right side with the blunt side of the craft knife for thin cardboard, and lightly with the sharp side for thicker cardboard.

Folding the box

1 Fold into a box along the score lines with all the tabs inside. Glue the two top tabs down over the side tabs. It is not necessary to glue the side tabs in place. Paper clips are excellent for holding the top tabs in place while they dry.

A Professional Finish

When gluing awkward objects, use paper clips to hold the layers together while the glue dries.

For a clean fold on a card, score the fold line first. With the blunt edge of a craft knife, score a line on the right side of the card. The idea is that you are not cutting the card, just indenting it.

On thick cardboard, score the fold line first to achieve a clean fold. With the sharp edge of a craft knife, lightly score a line on the right side of the cardboard. This will cut it just deep enough to allow the cardboard to fold easily.

This selection of boxes—of varying sizes and shapes—is within the scope of even a beginning handicrafter. Covered with fabric or paper, decorated with stencils, and tied with ribbon, they are dressed up enough to go to any party.

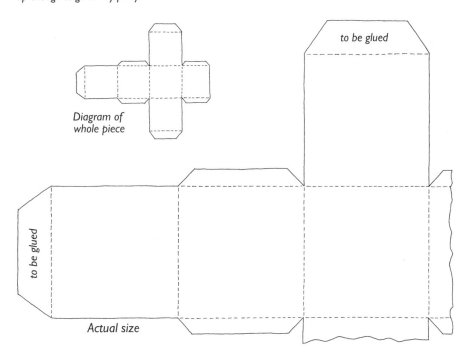

Diagram of whole piece

to be glued

to be glued

Actual size

To make a simple box, use this template, extending it to its complete shape using the small diagram as a guide. Note that there are seven tabs, three slightly larger (to be glued) and four smaller (no need to glue).

Make-It-Yourself Gifts

*At Christmas, add that personal touch by creating your own gifts
at home for family and friends. The following pages offer novel ideas for presents
that will be a pleasure to make and to give.*

Snappy Sneakers

*Turn plain canvas shoes and sneakers
into designer footwear with a few deft
strokes of a paintbrush. The quick-drying
acrylic paint is so easy to use that children can create and paint individually
designed shoes to give to their friends.*

WHAT YOU NEED

- ◆ Canvas shoes or sneakers
- ◆ artist's gesso
- ◆ artist's acrylic paints in a selection of colors
- ◆ paintbrushes: medium round and liner
- ◆ pencil
- ◆ newspaper
- ◆ fabric waterproofing spray

Preparing the shoes

1 Remove the shoelaces and make
sure the canvas is clean and free
from dust. If the shoes are not new,
or are marked in any way, you may
wish to coat the fabric with artist's
gesso, which will give a smooth,
clean surface for painting.
2 Stuff the shoes with newspaper so
that they will keep their shape while
you are painting the design.

HINT
Buy colored
or patterned
shoelaces
to match your
design colors.

Painting the shoes

1 On paper, sketch out the design
you want to use on the shoes, or copy
the design on the shoes in the photograph. When sketching your design,
consider the shape of the shoes and
make your design appropriate for the
contours of the shoes.
2 Lightly pencil the main features
of the design onto the canvas.
3 Paint the main design features
first, and then the background. If
the canvas shoes have rubber toe
pieces, paint them in solid colors.
4 When the paint is dry, use a liner
brush to add details.

Finishing the shoes

1 Allow the paint to dry thoroughly.
2 Spray the canvas shoes with fabric
waterproofing to protect them from
both dirt and water.
3 Remove the newspaper only
when waterproofing spray is
completely dry.
4 Rethread the shoelaces.

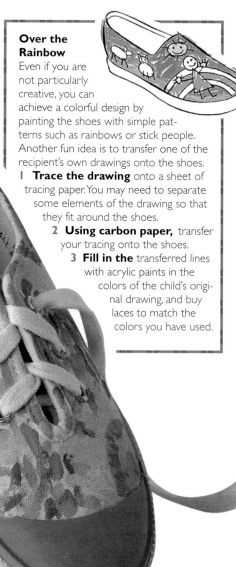

**Over the
Rainbow**
Even if you are
not particularly
creative, you can
achieve a colorful design by
painting the shoes with simple patterns such as rainbows or stick people.
Another fun idea is to transfer one of the
recipient's own drawings onto the shoes.
1 Trace the drawing onto a sheet of
tracing paper. You may need to separate
some elements of the drawing so that
they fit around the shoes.
2 Using carbon paper, transfer
your tracing onto the shoes.
3 Fill in the transferred lines
with acrylic paints in the
colors of the child's original drawing, and buy
laces to match the
colors you have used.

Bead Jewelry

Jewelry design is limited only by your imagination. With a selection of interesting beads and some basic equipment, you can make a gift that will delight any young person.

WHAT YOU NEED

- ✦ Selection of decorative beads of your choice
- ✦ wire cutters
- ✦ pliers: long-nosed, round-nosed
Necklace or bracelet
- ✦ nylon-coated wire (tiger tail), 2 inches longer than finished length of necklace or bracelet
- ✦ 2 crimps for each item
- ✦ barrel or ring clasp
Earrings
- ✦ 2 headpins for each pair of earrings
- ✦ 2 eyepins for each pair of earrings (for double-section earrings)
- ✦ screw-on or clip-on fittings, or pierced-ear wires

Making the necklace or bracelet

1 First thread a crimp onto one end of the wire, positioning it about ¾ inch from the end.

2 Take one half of the clasp and thread the short end of the wire through the loop of the clasp and then back through the crimp.

3 Making sure that the crimp and clasp are fitted snugly together, squeeze the crimp with the pliers until it locks the wire securely.

4 Thread the beads of your choice on to the wire, leaving the last 1¼ inches of wire free.

5 Thread the free end of the wire through the second crimp, then through the other half of the clasp and back through the crimp. Do not squeeze the crimp shut yet.

6 Push the excess wire back through the last two or three beads. Pull the end of the wire as tightly as possible, so that there are no gaps between beads, crimp and clasp. Squeeze the crimp firmly with the pliers to lock the wire in place. Carefully snip off any excess wire.

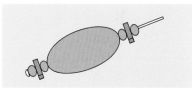

> **EXTRA LONG EARRINGS**
>
> - You can make really long earrings by adding a further eyepin threaded with one or more beads before you attach the earring fitting.
> - Try adding several eyepins, each threaded with a single bead for a different effect.
> - The wires may also be bent into interesting shapes to add variety to the designs.

Making the earrings

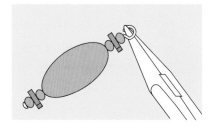

1 Thread the selected beads onto the headpin; leave the last ½ inch of wire bare. The headpin wire can be cut to any length, depending on how long you want the earrings to be.

2 With the long-nosed pliers, bend the end of the wire to make a slightly open loop.

3 Pass the loop through the hole on the earring clips or wires and close with the round-nosed pliers.

Painted Mat

Rather than opting for a ready-made floor mat, you can brighten a teenager's room with a mat you have painted yourself. Teenagers may like to make this gift themselves to give to friends.

WHAT YOU NEED

- ◆ 1 yard primed 10 ounce canvas, 60 inches wide, hemmed at the edges
- ◆ 2-yard fringing
- ◆ white acrylic house paint, flat or semi-gloss
- ◆ Jo Sonja (or Liquitex) artist's colors: yellow light, green oxide, jade, raw sienna, gold oxide, ultramarine, dioxazine purple, titanium white, naphthol crimson
- ◆ paintbrushes: 2-inch decorating, no. 12 round
- ◆ toothbrush
- ◆ metal spatula (or old table knife)
- ◆ water-based clear flat varnish
- ◆ white glue
- ◆ soft pencil

Preparing the canvas

1 Apply two coats of white acrylic house paint to the canvas. Let the paint to dry between coats.
2 Using a soft pencil, draw a 4-inch border around the edge of the mat. Sketch in the border design, following the painting guide or inventing your own pattern. The design looks most effective if the border has a free appearance rather than a precise geometrical look.

Making a Wall Hanging

This design could also be used to make a wall hanging, either the same size as the mat or somewhat smaller – simply scale down the elements of the design to suit whatever size of hanging you want to make.

Follow the instructions for making the painted mat, omitting the fringing at one end and making the hem at that end large enough to take a piece of strong, flat doweling about 4 inches longer than the width of the canvas. When the design is painted and finished, push the doweling through the wide hem and attach a strong cord for hanging. Trim with tassels if desired.

Painting guide — *The design illustrated is based on the shapes and colors of nuts and leaves. The border motif is created from abstract motifs and designs.*

However, this design and the colors specified are meant as suggestions only. The free style of painting used offers you plenty of scope for your own ideas. Before starting to paint the canvas, use wallpaper lining paper to experiment with color and design and develop your own style.

3 In the center area of the mat, sketch in nuts and leaves.

Painting the canvas

Leaves

1 Paint the leaves in green oxide, leaving a thin unpainted strip down the center of each leaf to represent the vein of the leaf. Allow to dry.

2 Dry-brush over the leaves with jade paint. This will add dimension, depth and light.

Nuts

1 Paint the nuts with gold oxide, leaving patches of canvas unpainted to create highlights.

2 Dry-brush the nuts in raw sienna to define and shape them.

Background

1 Leaving a ⅜-inch border around the nuts and leaves, lightly cover the background with ultramarine and allow to dry.

2 Dry-brush over the same area with dioxazine purple. In some places allow the colors to blend into each other, and in other places allow single colors to stand out.

3 Paint around each leaf and nut in yellow light, allowing the edges to blend into the blue paints.

Border

1 Following the painting guide, paint the border design. Paint the background to the design in green oxide.

2 Using a toothbrush and a spatula, spatter blue paint over the

mat by sliding the paint-loaded spatula across the mat and releasing the paint particles with light toothbrush strokes.

Finishing

1 When the paint has dried, apply two or three coats of clear varnish.

2 Coat the back of the mat with a mixture of one part white glue and one part water. Allow to dry.

3 If the fringing has not already been attached by the supplier of the canvas, stitch it to the ends of the mat.

> **HINT**
> *Ready-primed canvas bought from a sailmaker is the most economical material for this project. Heavy-duty canvas is difficult to sew, so ask the sailmaker to stitch the hems around the edges and attach the fringing to the short ends.*

Framed Memories

Photographs keep memories alive, and a montage of photographs celebrating a dear one's life makes a special and personal gift for a family member or a close friend.

WHAT YOU NEED

- ✦ Selection of photographs
- ✦ large picture frame
- ✦ mounting board, cut to fit the frame
- ✦ scalpel or craft knife
- ✦ ruler
- ✦ square
- ✦ jar lid or saucer, with a circumference large enough to frame several of the photographs
- ✦ invisible or masking tape
- ✦ sheet of rub-off decorative corners and borders
- ✦ hard pencil (or empty ballpoint pen)

Choosing the photographs

1 Select a series of images that are related thematically. You will need one main photograph, such as a large portrait, as a focal point for the arrangement. For the montage illustrated here, the focal point is a favorite photograph of the recipient's grandfather; the other images reflect various aspects of his life – his wife, his daughter, his home and his first car.

2 Experiment with the positions of the photographs on the mounting board until you are happy with the arrangement. Remember that symmetrical arrangements are the most pleasing to the eye.

3 Decide which images you would like to place in a circular opening. (Circular openings make excellent frames for displaying portraits, especially old black-and-white or sepia portrait photographs.)

Cutting the openings

1 Working on the back of the mounting board, mark the cutting lines for the frames with a pencil. Use a ruler and a square to mark the square-edged frames and an inverted jar lid or saucer of the appropriate size for the circular frames. You can cut each frame to display either the whole image or only part of it, but

the frame must be smaller than the photograph so that the photograph will sit behind the mounting board. Start by marking the frame for the focal image, and measure the distances between images carefully to keep them uniform.

2 With the scalpel or craft knife, cut out the frames. Cut the square-edged frames first, using the steel ruler. To cut out the circular frames, take the lid or saucer that you used to trace the shape and place it over the tracing. Gently score around the shape with the knife, as you would with a pencil. Remove the lid or saucer and cut out the circle along the score line. Work slowly and carefully and do not press the scalpel too hard.

Picture Frames

Select a large picture frame so that there will be enough space to display the photographs to the best advantage. The frame shown here is made of recycled wood, which suits the subject perfectly.

You can buy picture frames with holes already cut in various shapes in the mounting boards.

Mounting the photographs

1 When you have cut out all the frames, carefully fix the photographs in position with invisible tape or masking tape. Use only one piece of tape along the top edge of each photograph. This allows the photographic paper to expand and shrink with the weather, which prevents the photographs from wrinkling.

2 With the hard pencil, transfer the rub-on borders onto the mounting board around the photographs. Place them to accentuate the focal image and embellish the secondary images.

Finishing

1 Make sure that the glass is clean, and carefully fit the mounting board with the photographs into the picture frame. Secure the back of the frame according to the manufacturer's or frame-maker's instructions.

Hand-Covered Photograph Album

Here is a simple method of converting an inexpensive, purchased photograph album into a distinctive and useful gift.

WHAT YOU NEED

- ✦ Photograph album with spiral binding
- ✦ craft batting, a little larger all round than the complete cover (back and front) of the album
- ✦ fabric, 1½ inches larger all round than the complete album cover
- ✦ 1-yard ribbon, 1inch wide, to coordinate with fabric
- ✦ wrapping paper to coordinate with fabric
- ✦ sewing thread
- ✦ sewing needle
- ✦ tape measure
- ✦ scissors
- ✦ white glue
- ✦ clean scrap paper

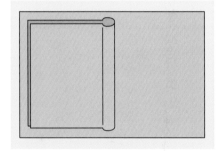

Applying the batting

1 Evenly coat the outside of the front cover of the album, including the edges and the spine, with a thin layer of white glue.

2 Lay the piece of batting flat and position the glued front cover of the album on it, with the edges just inside the edges of the batting.

3 Repeat step 1 for the outside back cover of the album.

4 Bring the batting over the spine, keeping it taut and smooth, and press it down over the glued back cover.

5 If necessary, trim the batting so that it will just wrap around the edges of the cover. Clip the corners so that they will not be bulky, and press the batting down onto the glued edges. Allow the glue to dry.

Covering the album

1 Cut the ribbon in half. With right sides facing, lay one piece of ribbon over the fabric with the end centered on one short edge of the fabric. Stitch a ¾ x 1¼-inch rectangle to hold the ribbon flat and secure.

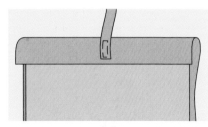

2 Repeat step 1 to attach the second piece of ribbon to the opposite edge of the fabric. Trim the ribbon ends at an angle to prevent fraying.

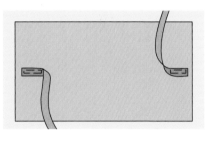

3 Open the album. On the inside cover, mark the center point of the vertical edge. Run glue along this edge from top to bottom. Press the wrong side of one short edge of the fabric onto the glued area, aligning the stitched end of the ribbon with the center point. Let the glue dry.

4 Turn the album over; repeat step 3 on the other side. Pull the fabric over the cover with the album nearly closed. Close the album; put sheets of paper between the cover and the pages in case of glue leakage. Let the glue dry thoroughly.

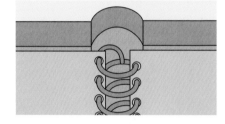

5 If necessary, trim the fabric at the spine so that it will tuck down flat behind the spiral binding. Glue the top and bottom of the inside of the spine and stick the fabric down.

6 Apply glue to the top and bottom edges of the inside front cover. Stick the fabric down, mitering the corners and ensuring that the fabric covers the outside of the album smoothly. Repeat this step on the inside back.

Finishing

1 To make endpapers, cut two pieces of wrapping paper ¼ inch smaller all round than the inside dimensions of the cover. Glue the endpapers to the insides of the covers to conceal the raw edges of the fabric.

2 When the glue is dry, close the album and tie the ribbon in a bow.

Handmade Hatboxes

These functional yet stylish fabric-covered boxes provide decorative storage for hats and other personal items.

> The measurements given first are for making the larger box, and those in brackets are for making the smaller box.

WHAT YOU NEED

- Heavy cardboard: A1sheet
- light cardboard: A1 sheet, A0 sheet
- 20-inch (12-inch) lightweight, firmly woven cotton fabric, 44 inches wide
- about 14 x 14-inch lightweight batting
- 1⅜-yard (2⅛-yard) braid
- 1⅜-yard cord, ⅜-inch diameter
- white glue
- pencil
- ruler
- compass
- scissors
- scalpel or craft knife
- wide masking tape
- spring clothespins

Cutting out the cardboard

1 Using the pencil, compass and scalpel, mark, label and cut the following shapes from the heavy cardboard: **A** one circle radius 6¼ inches (4½ inches) for the lid; **B** one circle radius 6 inches (4⅜ inches) for the base.

2 With the pencil, compass, ruler and scalpel, mark, label and cut the following shapes from the light cardboard: **C** one circle radius 6¼ inches (4½ inches) for the lid liner; **D** two circles radius 5¾ inches

(4¼ inches) for the base liners; **E** two strips 1¾ x 40 inches (1½ x 30 inches) for the lid rims; **F** one strip 1½ x 40 inches (1⅜ x 30 inches) for the lid rim liner; **G** one rectangle 7 x 39 inches (6¾ x 28¾ inches) for the base wall; **H** one strip 7 x 39 inches (6½ x 28¾ inches) for the base wall liner.

Constructing the lid

1 Apply a strip of masking tape along one edge of one lid rim (E), so that half the width of the tape overhangs the edge of the cardboard.

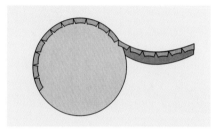

2 Cut V-shaped notches along the overhanging tape.

3 With the rim at right angles to the lid (A), roll the rim around the edge of the lid and attach it by pulling the notched masking tape onto the lid and pressing it firmly into place.

4 Overlap the ends of the rim and tape them together.

Covering the lid

1 Apply glue to the lid top and place it on the batting. Smooth out the batting and trim it to fit exactly.

2 Trace the outline of the lid onto

the wrong side of the fabric, adding a ⅝-inch seam allowance. Cut the traced shape from the fabric and notch the seam allowance.

3 Glue the fabric and place it over the batting, pulling it taut as you work. Glue the notched seam allowance down onto the rim.

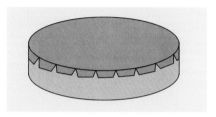

4 Trace the shape of the second lid rim (E) onto the wrong side of the fabric. Add a ⅝-inch seam allowance all around and cut out.

5 Glue the lid rim and place it on the wrong side of the fabric. Turn over and glue the seam allowance to the wrong side along one long edge only.

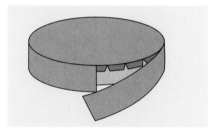

6 Glue the second rim over the first, with the glued-down seam allowance sitting over the notched lid cover. Trim one end so that the cardboard ends sit flush. Glue the remaining seam allowance over the join.

7 Glue the lower edge of the seam allowance to the inside of the rim. Clamp the fabric to the rim with clothespins until the glue has dried.

Lining the lid

1 Place the lid rim liner (F) on the wrong side of the fabric and trace around it, adding a ⅝-inch seam allowance. Cut out the traced shape from the fabric.

2 Glue the lid rim liner and place it on the wrong side of the cut-out fabric. Glue the ⅝-inch seam allow-

---

CUTTING THE CARDBOARD PIECES

Cut the fabric using the cardboard pieces as templates.

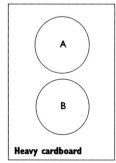

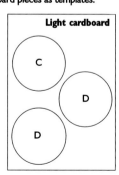

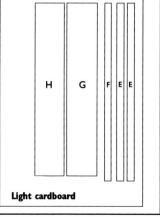

Heavy cardboard

Light cardboard

Light cardboard

3 Coat the base wall with glue and center it on the wrong side of the fabric. Roll the base wall along the fabric piece until it is covered, smoothing out any wrinkles as you go.

4 Glue the top seam allowance to the inside of the base wall.

5 Notch the seam allowance along the lower edge. Glue it to the base.

Attaching the cord handles

1 Using sharp scissors, pierce two holes in the base wall, opposite each other and about 2 inches from the top.

2 Measure and cut enough cord to form a handle running from hole to hole across the top of the box. Thread the ends of the cord through the holes from the outside and hold them in place by gluing and taping them flat to the inside of the box.

Lining the base

1 Place the base liners (D) on the wrong side of the fabric and trace around them, adding a ⅜-inch seam allowance. Cut out the traced shapes from the fabric.

2 Working on one at a time, coat the base liners with glue and place them on the wrong sides of the fabric circles. Notch the seam allowances and glue them to the wrong sides of the cardboard liners.

3 Glue one of the covered base liners to the outside of the base of the box and the other to the inside.

4 Trace around the base wall liner (H) on the wrong side of the fabric, adding a ⅜-inch seam allowance. Cut the traced shape from the fabric.

5 Glue the base wall liner to the wrong side of the cut-out fabric. Turn and glue the seam allowance to the wrong side along the upper and lower edges. Trim off the seam allowance at one short end.

6 Glue the wrong side of the liner and fit it inside the box, pressing it into place. Lap the remaining seam allowance over the join. Hold the liner against the base wall with clothespins until the glue dries.

ance to the wrong side along both long edges. Glue the covered lid rim liner to the inside of the lid rim. Trim one end to fit snugly and glue the seam allowance over the join.

3 Trace around the lid liner (C) on the wrong side of the fabric, adding a ⅝-inch seam allowance. Cut out the traced shape from the fabric.

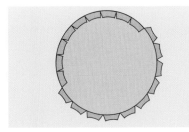

4 Glue the lid liner and place it on the wrong side of the cut-out fabric. Notch the seam allowance and glue it around the edge of the lid liner. Glue the liner to the inside of the lid.

5 Glue the braid around the outside edge of the rim.

Making and covering the base

1 Trace the shape of the base wall (G) onto the wrong side of the fabric. Add ⅝ inch all around for the seam allowance. Cut out the traced shape.

2 Join the base wall (G) to the base (B) in the same way as you joined the lid rim to the lid. Overlap the ends of the wall and secure with masking tape.

Luxury Handkerchief Bag

You can use remnants to make this quick and easy fabric bag for storing handkerchiefs, stockings, scarves or luxury soaps. Put a miniature bottle of perfume and some lace-edged handkerchiefs inside it to complete your gift.

WHAT YOU NEED

- 10 x 32-inch heavy upholstery fabric (chintz, tapestry or damask)
- 10 x 24-inch silk lining fabric
- 1-yard-thick silk upholstery cord, in a shade to tone with the fabric
- sewing thread to match the fabric
- tape measure
- dressmaking pins
- sewing needle
- sewing machine

Making the bag

1 Use the sewing machine to zigzag around the raw edges of upholstery fabric to prevent fraying.
2 Fold the fabric in half widthwise with the right sides together, and

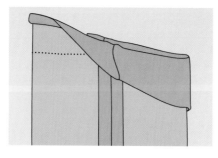

straight machine stitch the sides together with a ⅜-inch seam allowance. Press the seams open.
3 To make a deep hem along the top edge, fold the top raw edge over ⅜ inch to the wrong side and press. Fold over a further 3½ inches to the wrong side and slipstitch in place.

Variations

Adapt the bag for storing soap, perfume or cosmetics by lining it with shower curtain fabric instead of silk.
The bag can also contain an inner bag filled with potpourri, and can be hung in closets or from door handles or tucked in among cushions. Make a sachet of tulle to fit into the bag, leaving a small opening in one side. Turn the sachet right side out, fill it with potpourri, and close the opening with slipstitch. Place the sachet in the bag and tie the cord. Sew a fabric loop to the bag for hanging.

Making the lining

1 Using the lining fabric, proceed as for previous steps 1 and 2.
2 At the top, turn down a ⅜-inch double hem to the wrong side. Sew it down by slipstitch or machine.

Assembling the bag

1 Turn the bag right side out and leave the lining wrong side out.
2 Insert the lining into the bag and baste it into place just below where the large hem folds over. Slipstitch the lining to the inside of the bag,

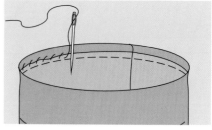

easing it to fit if necessary. Remove the basting stitches.
3 Fold the upholstery cord in half and mark the mid-point. Measure 3½ inches down from the top of the bag along a side seam and stitch the mid-point of the cord to the side seam. Bring the cord to the other side of the bag and tie it in a bow.

NOTE
It is important to neaten the raw edges by zigzagging or overlocking them because heavy upholstery fabric often has a complex weave that frays easily.

Easy Mothball Bags

A cluster of mothball bags is a great present. The bags are quick and easy to make, and are an excellent way of using up those odd scraps of cotton fabric that are too pretty to throw away.

WHAT YOU NEED

- ◆ 3 scraps printed cotton fabric, 8 x 8 inch
- ◆ 2-yard lace edging, ³⁄₈ inch wide
- ◆ 2¹⁄₂-yard ribbon, ¹⁄₈ inch wide
- ◆ sewing thread to match the fabric
- ◆ mothballs or naphthalene
- ◆ scissors
- ◆ pinking shears (optional)
- ◆ sewing needle or sewing machine
- ◆ tape measure

Preparing the fabric

1 Cut three 8-inch-diameter circles from the fabric scraps.

2 To prevent the raw edges from fraying, neaten them by hand or by machine with zigzag stitch, or trim them with pinking shears.

Attaching the lace

1 Cut the lace into lengths the measurement of the circumference of the circles plus ³⁄₈ inch, and pin it around the circles so that it overlaps the edge of the fabric. Stitch it to the fabric.

2 Run small gathering stitches ³⁄₄ inches in from the edge of each circle.

Assembling the bags

1 Place a little pile of mothballs (or naphthalene flakes) in the center of each circle, and then close the bags by carefully pulling the gathering threads. Tie the threads securely.

2 Tie a length of ribbon around the top of each bag to cover the gathering.

3 Tie the three bags together with ribbon and stitch the ends of the ribbon to make a loop for hanging.

> **NOTE**
> *Mothballs (or naphthalene flakes) can be dangerous if swallowed. Fasten the bags securely so that the contents cannot fall out, and keep the bags out of reach of children.*

Printed T-shirts

You don't have to be an artist to create eye-catching T-shirt designs—all you need is access to a photocopier and a good eye for suitable images. You can photocopy the images on this page. Enlarge or reduce the images to fit the size of your T-shirt.

WHAT YOU NEED

- T-shirts
- images to photocopy
- photocopy acetate
- turpentine
- fabric paints: red, blue, yellow, black
- tablespoon
- paintbrushes: medium round, small liner
- adhesive tape
- chopping board
- old tea towel
- old towel
- iron
- plate

Preparing the images

1 Any illustration or photograph is suitable for printing on a T-shirt, so long as it photocopies well in black and white and the image is clear with good lines and shading.

2 Photocopy the image, enlarging or reducing until you have a size appropriate to the size of the T-shirt. It is best to make the copies fairly dark.

3 If you want to include text with the picture, you need to make a mirror image of the writing so that it prints the correct way on the fabric. To make a mirror image, photocopy the image on acetate

---

Hints

For added interest, put smaller versions of the image onto the sleeves or back of the shirt.

Center the image on the top two-thirds of the T-shirt so that it is shown to its best advantage. Remember that the bottom of a T-shirt is often tucked into jeans or a skirt.

Practice on an old T-shirt or other fabric scrap first until you have perfected the technique.

---

film. Then place the sheet of acetate back to front on the photocopier glass and photocopy the reversed image onto a sheet of paper.

Fixing the images onto the T-shirt

1 Lay the T-shirt on an old towel on a flat working surface. Have the turpentine, tablespoon, adhesive tape, photocopies and paintbrush within easy reach.

2 Wrap an old tea towel around a chopping board and secure it with some tape. Place the wrapped board inside the T-shirt, beneath where you plan to place the design. This provides a firm, slightly absorbent surface against

---

which to apply the photocopied design, and prevents the dye running through to the other side of the shirt.

3 Cut around the photocopied image, leaving at least ¾ inch of blank paper all around. Place the photocopy face down on the T-shirt and secure it with adhesive tape, taking care not to cover any of the design.

4 Paint turpentine over the back of the image until it is saturated. You should be able to see the image through the paper quite clearly, but there should be no pools of liquid on the surface.

5 Rub firmly all over the image area with the back of the spoon, holding the paper and T-shirt down securely as you go so that the image doesn't move around. Go over the whole area about three times. If the turpentine evaporates before you have finished, reapply and continue rubbing.

6 Lift one corner of the paper to see whether the image has transferred to the fabric. If you can see any areas that are missing, replace the corner and rub the entire image again. With experience you will be able to judge the correct degree of pressure, rubbing and saturation of turpentine to achieve the best effect.

7 Remove the paper carefully, starting from one corner and slowly peeling it back. Some makes of T-shirt are slightly fluffier than others; if any pieces of blackened fluff appear as you peel the paper back, pick them off the surface with your

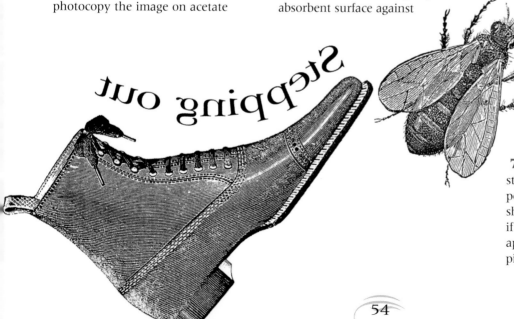

fingers or a brush. If fragments land on clean areas of the shirt, don't remove them until the turpentine has evaporated.

8 To fix the image, iron the shirt at a temperature suitable for the fabric.

Applying the color

1 Decide what colors to use on the images. Place the chopping board behind the images to protect the other side of the shirt.

2 Mix the fabric paints on a plate with a small amount of water. It is a good idea to experiment on scraps of fabric first until you have a good consistency. If the paint is too runny, the color will "bleed" over the edges of the image. If the paint is too dry, it will create a rough, caked-on effect.

3 Paint the images by filling in different areas with flat colors and outlining the image with a small liner brush.

4 Follow the manufacturer's instructions for fixing the paints and washing.

Candles With Pressed Flowers

Using pressed flowers from the garden and a little imagination, you can create beautiful candles as gifts for Christmas. Several candles grouped together make an ideal centerpiece for a dinner table .

WHAT YOU NEED

+ Flowers and foliage
+ beeswax candles
+ white glue
+ white paraffin wax
+ heat-proof container, deep enough to submerge the candles in
+ saucepan, large enough to stand the container in
+ cooking thermometer
+ tweezers
+ swizzle stick or small paintbrush

Decorating the candles

1 Using a swizzle stick or small paintbrush, apply a spot of glue to the back of the pressed flower that is to be the focal point of your decoration.

2 Carefully pick up the flower with the tweezers and position it on the candle. Press it gently into place with your fingers.

3 Add more flowers or leaves around the focal point until you are satisfied with the design. You can slip some of the plant material behind the focal flower so that it remains at the front of the design.

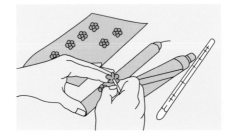

Hints

Before you place your plant material on the candle, draw an outline of the candle on paper and place the plant material on this, rearranging the design until you are happy with it.

It is a good idea to keep a main part of your design near the bottom of the candle, so that it is not lost so quickly when the lighted candle melts down.

Don't throw away unused paraffin wax; let it solidify and put it aside to use later.

Sealing the flowers onto the candles

1 Put the paraffin wax in the heat-proof container. Place the container in a saucepan of water and heat the water until the paraffin wax melts.

2 Put the thermometer into the paraffin wax and, when it reaches 180°F.–200°F., hold the candle by the wick and submerge it in the molten wax. Wait five seconds before you lift the candle out.

3 Allow the excess wax to drip off, then stand the candle upright. Leave the paraffin wax to cool and harden.

CAUTION

Do not apply direct heat to the paraffin wax, as it is extremely flammable if overheated.

Aromatic Beeswax Candles

Make these candles to set the mood for a special occasion. Beeswax is long-burning and does not drip, and when the candles are lit they will fill the room with the delicious scent of natural honey.

WHAT YOU NEED

- Sheets of preformed beeswax
- length of braided wick, 1/8 inch wide
- ruler
- large pair of scissors
- hair dryer (in cold weather)

Making the candles

1 Experiment with the shapes and sizes of the candles by cutting out sheets of thin, pliable cardboard and rolling them up in various ways.

2 When you are satisfied with the shape you have achieved, unroll and flatten the cardboard, place it on a beeswax sheet and cut carefully around it. To increase the thickness, add more sheets of wax.

3 Cut a piece of wick ¾ inch longer than the finished candle.

4 You may need to soften the beeswax slightly to make it pliable and to prevent the sheet from cracking as you roll. To soften the beeswax, wave a hair dryer over the sheet for about 10 seconds or leave the beeswax near a sunny window for about 10 minutes.

5 Lay the softened beeswax flat on a clean surface. Pinch off a small piece of the wax from the place where you will begin to roll and set it aside. Place the wick along the edge of the sheet and push it gently into the wax.

6 Turn the edge of the sheet over the wick to make a small fold and press lightly to encase the wick.

7 Using the palms of both hands, roll the wax away from you with a light but even pressure, making sure that the base of the candle is level so that it will sit flat when it is finished.

Hints

When they are alight, beeswax candles give off a natural honeylike fragrance. However, if you would like to add a special scent to the candles, use an eye dropper to drop fragrant oil onto the wick before you roll the beeswax. A small candle requires three or four drops, and a large one between 10 and 20 drops.

Candle Shapes

Tapered candles

To achieve an attractive tapered look, trim one side of the sheet diagonally and roll from the long end.

Square candles

To make a square candle, place a ruler close to the edge of the beeswax sheet and turn the wax around it. Repeat this step each time you turn the sheet.

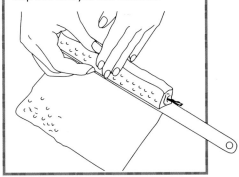

8 Continue rolling more sheets of beeswax around the first until the candle is the thickness you want. Press the outside edge of the wax against the candle to prevent it from unrolling.

9 If the shape has become a little distorted because of uneven pressure when rolling, you can make the candle perfectly cylindrical by rolling it briskly back and forth a few times.

Finishing

1 Trim the wick to ½ inch and pinch the piece of reserved wax around the base of the wick. This will help it to light more easily.

2 As a final touch to the gift, group a few candles of complementary shapes and include a box of luxury matches.

Braided Leather Belt

Make this beautiful belt from good-quality leather, and it will last for years. The design is suitable for either a man or a woman, or the belt could be made for both to share.

WHAT YOU NEED

- ✦ Strip of leather, 1⅜ inches wide x about 60 inches long
- ✦ matching strip of leather, 1 inch wide x 5 inches long
- ✦ solid metal belt buckle, to fit belt 1⅜ inches wide
- ✦ black leather dye
- ✦ small, stiff sponge brush
- ✦ pencil
- ✦ long steel ruler
- ✦ craft knife or utility knife, suitable for cutting leather
- ✦ access to shoemaker or leather worker (for assembling and stitching the belt)

Preparing the leather

1 Ensure that the edges of the long leather strip are perfectly straight and even. Trim them with the craft knife or utility knife if necessary.

2 On the wrong side of the leather, mark off 13¾ inches at each end. In the center of the strip, between the marks, carefully measure and mark six parallel lines ³⁄₁₆ inch apart along the strip.

3 Use the craft or utility knife to cut along the lines. At one end, start the inner four cuts ¾ inch in from the outer two (this is the buckle end). At the other end, start the outer two cuts 1¼ inches in from the inner pair

---

Buckling Up

Select a buckle heavy enough to match the belt and, as a general rule, choose a plain design if the belt is for a man and a more elaborate one for a woman.
The buckle illustrated is of brass bound with a narrow strip of fine, soft leather, but plain metal would look equally good. The buckle must be made of solid, heavy metal – plastic or cheap, soft metal will not last.

---

of cuts, and the cuts between ¾ inch in from the inner two cuts (this is the tongue end).

4 Using the sponge brush, carefully apply black leather dye to all the cut edges of the leather strip. Allow the dye to dry thoroughly.

Making the braid

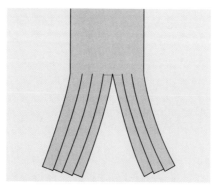

1 Working from the buckle end, divide the cut portion of the belt into four strips on the left and three strips on the right.

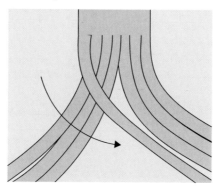

2 Draw the outer left-hand strip over the three other left-hand strips to the right-hand side.

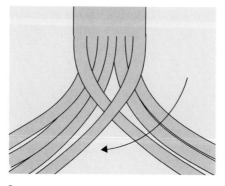

3 Draw the outer right-hand strip over the two other right-hand strips

and the strip that was originally on the outer left.

4 Repeat steps 2 and 3 until you have braided in all seven strips once, finishing with a step 2. Each time, you will draw the outer strip over three strips to the opposite side of the belt.

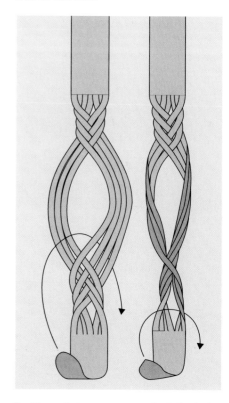

5 Thread the tongue end of the belt through the upper gap between the braided strips, from front to back. Then thread the tongue end of the belt through the lower gap between the strips, again from front to back.

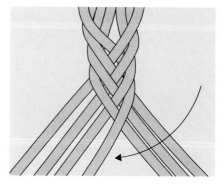

6 To braid the second sequence of seven strips, draw the outer right-hand strip over to the opposite side of the belt.

7 Proceed as for the first braiding sequence, drawing strips over alternately from side to side until you have braided in all seven strips. Repeat step 5 to complete the sequence.

8 Repeat the whole sequence until the complete braid is formed.

Assembling the belt

To put the belt together, you will need to find a shoemaker or leather worker with equipment to punch the holes, attach the loop and buckle to the belt and add any decorative stitching you require.

1 Using the craft knife or utility knife, taper the tongue end of the belt. At the buckle end, mark a point 8 inches from the braid and cut an oval hole ³⁄₄ inch long for the prong of the buckle.

2 Using the black leather dye and the sponge brush, dye the cut edges of the hole, the cut edges of the tapered tongue end, and the cut edges of the 4³⁄₄-inch strip of leather.

3 Ask the shoemaker to stitch the 4³⁄₄-inch strip of leather into a loop that will fit the belt, trimming off any excess. Slide the loop over the buckle end of the belt.

4 Work the oval hole over the prong of the buckle and ask the shoemaker to stitch down the short end of leather to the wrong side to secure the buckle, trimming off any excess.

5 Ask the shoemaker to punch six holes 1 inch apart along the tongue end in the correct positions for the recipient's waist measurement.

6 If you want decorative stitching, get the shoemaker to stitch your desired pattern along the edges of the unbraided sections of the belt.

Trinket Box

Transform a wooden box into an appealing reminder of a wonderful time spent at the seashore. The box can be used to store buttons, paperclips or small trinkets and treasures.

WHAT YOU NEED

- ✦ Small wooden box
- ✦ shells of varying shapes, sizes and colors
- ✦ artist's acrylic paints: aqua, yellow, white
- ✦ paint palette
- ✦ natural sea sponge or scrunched-up rag
- ✦ hot glue gun and glue sticks
- ✦ clear gloss varnish
- ✦ small paintbrush

Preparation

1 Wash the shells thoroughly in a bucket of warm soapy water, rinse them well and allow them to dry.
2 Sort the shells into three sizes: small, medium and large.
3 On the paint palette, mix a small amount of aqua paint with a little white to make a mid-aqua shade. Take up a little of the paint on a damp sponge and apply it to the interior and the sides of the box. Sponging creates a soft, lightly textured effect.
4 When the first coat is dry, mix a lighter shade of aqua and apply a second, more sparing coat so that the mid-aqua is still visible. When this coat is dry, add a little white to the yellow to make a pale straw color, and apply delicate highlights here and there with the sponge.

Decorating the lid

1 Arrange the large shells and the medium-sized shells on the lid of the box, placing the largest in the center and using contrasting shapes, forms and colors as secondary

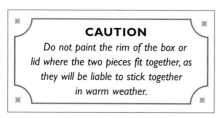

CAUTION

Do not paint the rim of the box or lid where the two pieces fit together, as they will be liable to stick together in warm weather.

points of interest. Move the shells around until you are satisfied with the effect.

2 Heat the glue gun and glue the shells in place, working from the center of the lid toward the edges. To create a natural effect, the shells should be overlapped and butted together in an irregular fashion until the lid is covered.
3 Use the smaller shells to fill the crevices. You can also create interest by gluing groups of smaller shells onto larger ones.

Finishing

Coat the shells with clear gloss varnish to seal them and give a glossy finish.

Romantic Flowers in a Pot

Flowers are a lovely gift for a friend or a sweetheart. Plant their favorite flower in this decorated pot, and your gift will be a charming reminder of your devotion.

WHAT YOU NEED

+ Terra-cotta flowerpot
+ small flowering plants
+ potting soil, enough to fill your pot
+ suitable images from wrapping paper, books or greeting cards
+ artist's gesso
+ white glue
+ wallpaper paste
+ artist's acrylic gloss medium (sealer)
+ polyurethane gloss varnish
+ Blu-Tack
+ paintbrushes: 2 small (for gluing and sealing), 7/8 inch imitation sable (for varnishing)
+ wet-and-dry sandpaper: no. 80
+ rubber sanding block
+ rubber roller
+ pieces of thick kitchen sponge
+ fine, curved scissors
+ pencil

Preparing the surfaces and applying the images

1 Sand all surfaces of the flowerpot lightly with sandpaper.
2 Apply a coat of artist's gesso to the outside of the pot. Allow the gesso to dry, then sandpaper the surface again. Seal the inside and outside surfaces with artist's acrylic medium.
3 Plan where you will put your images by fixing them to the pot with Blu-Tack and rearranging them until you are satisfied with the design. Trim the images with sharp scissors if necessary. Remove the images and lightly mark their positions on the pot.
4 Seal the images on both sides with artist's acrylic medium. Be careful not to make the coat of sealer too heavy, as the images may then become less pliable, so that it will be difficult to mold them around the pot. Allow the images to dry thoroughly.

Fixing the images

1 Taking one image at a time, apply a mixture of three parts wallpaper paste and one part white glue to the pot where the image is to go, and a small amount to the right side of the image.
2 Massage and mold the image into the surface, adding more glue if necessary. Roll over the image with the rubber roller to get rid of any lumps of glue or air bubbles. Remove the excess glue with a wet sponge.
3 Repeat steps 1 and 2 until all the images are in place.
4 Apply two coats of artist's acrylic medium to the surface, allowing

> **NOTE**
> Remember to choose plants that are suitable for the conditions in which they will be grown.

each coat to dry thoroughly before applying the next.

Finishing

1 Apply at least two coats of varnish, allowing the first coat to dry before applying the next. Leave the pot to dry thoroughly.
2 Fill the pot with potting soil and plant the flower according to the instructions supplied by the nursery.

Fragrant Potpourri

Fill pillows and sachets with your own potpourri mixtures, in combinations to suit a particular recipient's likes and dislikes, to give an added personal touch to this gift.

WHAT YOU NEED

+ Fragrant flowers and leaves, spices, orange peel (see individual recipes in section 3, below)
+ scissors
+ sheets of newspaper
+ shoe-box with lid, or large paper bag

Preparing the dried flowers and leaves

1 Gather flowers and leaves from the garden early in the morning (but after the overnight dew has dried, because damp plant material may rot). Pick flowers when they are fully open and before they begin to decay. Pick herbs just as they come into flower.

2 As soon as possible after picking, spread the flowers and leaves on several sheets of newspaper. Leave small flowers, such as tiny rosebuds, daisies or lavender, intact. To prepare larger flowers, remove the petals from the sepals (the green part at the base of the flower). Snip large leaves into several pieces with scissors.

3 Place the newspaper in a dry, airy place, away from wind and direct sunlight. Each day, toss the flowers with your fingertips to make sure that they dry out evenly. The material should be ready in three or four days.

4 When they are leathery to the touch, store the dried flowers and leaves in a lidded shoe-box or closed paper bag until you are ready to make the potpourri. This protects the plant material from dust and prevents it from becoming moldy.

Making the potpourri

1 Put the ingredients for the recipe you want to make in a box or paper bag and shake them together lightly.

2 Fill sachets or pillows with the mixture as soon as possible, and stitch or tie the receptacle shut.

Recipes

Mixed flowers
½ cup mixed heavily scented dried flower petals
¼ cup dried lavender
¼ cup dried lemon verbena leaves
¼ cup dried rosemary
Peel of one orange, cut into slivers and dried

Sweet rose
1 cup dried scented rose petals
Peel of half an orange, cut into slivers and dried
¼ cup crushed cloves and cinnamon sticks
¼ teaspoon nutmeg

Rose and herb
¼ cup dried scented rose petals
¼ cup dried mint
¼ cup dried lemon balm
¼ cup dried lemon verbena

NOTE

To crush cloves, place them in a plastic bag and roll gently with a rolling pin.

Crush leaves with your fingers to release the scent before placing them in the sachet.

Unless the dried material you have chosen is heavily scented (such as scented varieties of lavender, orange blossom, lemon verbena, rosemary, and some of the old-fashioned roses), you will need to add spices, herbs or citrus peel to intensify the fragrance.

You can buy scented oils to boost the fragrance, but this type of potpourri is not suitable for clothing and linen sachets or for sleep pillows, as the oil will seep through and stain the fabric.

Other potpourri ingredients include mimosa, jasmine, apple blossom, chamomile, sweet pea, narcissus, honeysuckle, and peel of lemon or lime.

Lemon verbena
1 cup dried lemon verbena

Old English lavender
1 cup dried very fragrant lavender
5 or 6 crushed cloves

Lavender and rose
½ cup dried fragrant lavender
½ cup dried rose petals
¼ cup dried lemon verbena leaves or dried thyme
10 crushed cloves, or a small stick of crushed cinnamon

Lavender and rosemary
½ cup dried rosemary
½ cup dried lavender
Some slivers of dried orange peel
8 whole cloves

Herb
1 cup dried rosemary
1 cup dried fragrant pine needles

Citrus potpourri
½ cup lemon verbena leaves
½ cup rose geranium leaves
Slivers of orange and lemon peel
10 crushed coriander seeds

Spicy Pomander

For a deliciously perfumed room or wardrobe, you can substitute pomanders for potpourri sachets.

1 Stud a few oranges or apples (or both) with whole cloves.

2 In a bowl, mix together ground spices – for example, cloves, cinnamon, nutmeg and orrisroot.

3 Roll the fruits in the ground spices until they are well covered.

4 Place the fruits in individual paper bags for several weeks to dry out.

5 When the fruits are dry, dust them off. Thread a ribbon through them for hanging in a wardrobe, or arrange them in a decorative bowl.

Festive Fare

TANTALIZE YOUR TASTE BUDS WITH TASTY TRADITIONAL AND INNOVATIVE DISHES

Marvellous Main Dishes

At the Christmas dinner table, roast turkey is an indispensible main dish.

Holiday Roast Turkey with Old-Fashioned Corn Bread Stuffing

Old-fashioned cooks sometimes added eggs and baking powder to their corn bread stuffing to give it a fluffier texture. The stuffing in this recipe is a delicious example.

- ✦ 3 tablespoons butter or margarine
- ✦ 1 large yellow onion, chopped
- ✦ 5 cups crumbled corn bread
- ✦ 5 cups toasted fresh bread crumbs
- ✦ 1 teaspoon baking powder
- ✦ 1 teaspoon poultry seasoning
- ✦ ¼ teaspoon black pepper
- ✦ ¾ cup lower-sodium chicken broth
    (recipe, opposite page)
- ✦ 1 large egg, lightly beaten
- ✦ 1 fresh or frozen and thawed turkey
    (12 pounds)
- ✦ 1 tablespoon vegetable oil
- ✦ Giblet Gravy (recipe, opposite page)

1 In a medium-size saucepan, melt the butter over moderate heat. Add the onion and cook for 5 minutes or until tender. Remove from the heat. In a large bowl, combine the corn bread, bread crumbs, baking powder, poultry seasoning, and pepper. Stir in the onion mixture. In a small bowl, whisk together broth and egg. Stir into the corn bread mixture. Toss to coat well.

2 Preheat oven to 325°F. Rinse turkey; drain and pat dry. Remove neck and giblets; set aside to make the Giblet Gravy. Stuff and truss turkey (see tip, page 71). Place, breast side up, on a rack in a large roasting pan. Brush with oil. Insert roasting thermometer in turkey thigh without touching bone. Spoon remaining stuffing into a lightly greased 2-quart casserole; cover and refrigerate.

3 Roast turkey for 3 to 3½ hours or until the thermometer registers 180°F., basting often and covering with foil to prevent overbrowning if necessary. Bake the covered casserole of stuffing alongside turkey during the last 30 minutes of roasting, adding an additional 2 to 3 tablespoons chicken broth if stuffing is dry. Let turkey stand for 15 to 20 minutes before carving.

4 Meanwhile, cook neck and giblets for Giblet Gravy. Reserve 2 tablespoons of the pan drippings from roast turkey for Giblet Gravy. Prepare gravy. Carve turkey, discarding skin (tip, right). Serve turkey and dressing with gravy. Makes 12 servings.

PREP TIME: 20 MINUTES COOKING TIME: 6 MINUTES
ROASTING TIME: 3 HOURS STANDING TIME: 15 MINUTES

Giblet Gravy

Rinse the turkey **neck** and **giblets**. Refrigerate the liver. In a large saucepan, combine the remaining giblets, neck, and 4 cups water. Add **1 medium-size yellow onion, cut into wedges; 1 large carrot, cut into chunks; 2 sprigs parsley; ½ teaspoon salt;** and **¼ teaspoon white or black pepper.** Bring to a boil. Lower the heat and simmer, covered, for 40 minutes. Add liver. Continue cooking for 20 minutes more or until tender. Strain broth, reserving 1⅓ cups. Reserve giblets and neck; discard vegetables. When cool enough to handle, remove meat from neck; discard neck bones. Finely chop the neck meat and giblets; set aside.

In a Dutch oven, whisk together reserved pan drippings, **1 can (12 ounces) evaporated skimmed milk, ⅓ cup all-purpose flour, ¼ teaspoon salt,** and **¼ teaspoon white or black pepper.** Cook over moderate heat until bubbly. Add the reserved broth. Cook, whisking constantly, until the mixture starts to thicken. Cook and whisk for 2 minutes more or until thickened. Stir in neck meat and giblets; heat through. Makes 3 cups.

Lower-Sodium Chicken Broth

When your recipe calls for a lower-sodium chicken broth, you have these options

✦ **Canned Broth Mix** You can mix ready-to-serve canned chicken broth with equal parts water and create a broth that has about 400 mg. to 450 mg. per cup. Or, look for canned lower-sodium chicken broth—it has about 550 mg. sodium per cup.

✦ **Bouillon Granules** Use low-sodium chicken bouillon granules broths with around 5 mg. and 0 mg. of sodium per cup.

How to Carve a Turkey

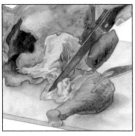 

1. To remove one leg, pull drumstick away from the body and cut between the thigh and the body. Cut through the joint that connects the thighbone to back. Repeat with the other leg. To separate each thigh from each drumstick, cut through joint that connects the thigh to drumstick.

2. Remove the wings by cutting through the joints where the wing bones are attached to the back. Carve the breast meat into thin slices. (The slices still will be attached at the bottom.)

 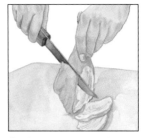

3. Loosen the breast meat slices by making a cut horizontally into the breast. To serve the remainder of the breast, cut smaller slices following the arc of the breastbone on each side of the bird.

4. If you want to slice the meat from the drumsticks, hold the drumstick upright, large end down. Slice the meat parallel to the bone, working the knife under the tendons. Rotate the leg, as necessary to get even slices.

Turkey Pot Pie

Turkey Pot Pie

When it comes to making tempting turkey pot pies, just follow this traditional rule—anything goes. Some old-time cooks topped their pies with dumplings. Others used pastry as in this recipe.

- ✦ 1½ pounds turkey tenderloin steaks, cut into 1-inch pieces
- ✦ 1 large potato, peeled and cubed
- ✦ 2 medium-size carrots, sliced
- ✦ 1 medium-size yellow onion, halved and thinly sliced
- ✦ ½ cup water
- ✦ ¼ teaspoon salt
- ✦ 1 can (12 ounces) evaporated skimmed milk
- ✦ ⅓ cup all-purpose flour
- ✦ 1 teaspoon dried thyme leaves
- ✦ ¼ teaspoon each salt and white or black pepper
- ✦ 1 store-bought or homemade pie crust
- ✦ Low-fat (1% milkfat) milk

1 Rinse turkey; drain and pat dry. In a large saucepan, place the turkey, potato, carrots, onion, water, and ¼ teaspoon salt. Bring to a boil. Lower the heat and simmer, covered, for 15 minutes or until the turkey is cooked through. Drain, reserving the cooking liquid.

2 Preheat the oven to 350°F. In the same saucepan, whisk together the evaporated skimmed milk, flour, thyme, ¼ teaspoon salt and pepper. Stir in the reserved cooking liquid. Cook over moderate heat, whisking constantly, until the mixture starts to thicken. Cook and whisk for 2 minutes more or until thickened and bubbly. Stir in the turkey mixture.

3 Spoon the turkey mixture into a lightly greased 2-quart casserole. Place the pie crust on top of mixture in a casserole (tip, opposite). Trim to 1 inch beyond edge of casserole. Fold under extra crust and crimp edge. Cut slits in crust. Brush with a little milk. Bake for 20 to 25 minutes or until pie crust is golden. Let stand for 5 minutes before serving. Makes 6 servings.

**PREP TIME: 20 MINUTES COOKING TIME: 25 MINUTES
BAKING TIME: 20 MINUTES STANDING TIME: 5 MINUTES**

Turkey Hash

Versatile cooks know how to make a hash from finely chopped leftover meat and potatoes. This tasty version features day-after turkey from a Christmas feast.

- ✦ 2 medium-size potatoes, peeled and chopped
- ✦ 2 tablespoons butter or margarine
- ✦ 1 medium-size yellow onion, chopped
- ✦ 1 small sweet green or red pepper, chopped
- ✦ 2 cups chopped cooked turkey
- ✦ ½ teaspoon dried rosemary leaves
- ✦ ¼ teaspoon black pepper
- ✦ ⅛ teaspoon salt
- ✦ ¼ cup lower-sodium chicken broth (page 67)

1 In a small saucepan, cover potatoes with water. Bring to a boil over high heat. Lower the heat and simmer, covered, for 15 minutes or until potatoes are tender. Drain.

2 In a 10-inch skillet, melt butter over moderate heat. Add the onion and green pepper and cook for 5 minutes or until tender. Stir in potatoes, turkey, rosemary, black pepper, and salt. Cook, stirring constantly, for 5 minutes. Stir in chicken broth. Cook and stir for 2 minutes more or until hash is desired consistency. Makes 3 servings.

PREP TIME: **20** MINUTES   COOKING TIME: **33** MINUTES

Moving Pie Crust With Ease

Positioning rolled-out homemade pie crust on top of a pie can sometimes be tricky. Here's how to move the pie crust without tearing it.

 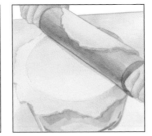

1. Transfer the pie crust to a rolling pin by lifting the edge of the crust over the top of the rolling pin. Then, gently roll up the crust.

2. After positioning the rolling pin at one edge of the filled casserole, slowly unroll the crust over the casserole.

Turkey Loaf with Mushroom Sauce

In bygone days when serving turkey was considered a splurge, women made this conforting dish to use up the precious leftovers.

For the turkey loaf:
- ✦ 2 cups finely chopped cooked turkey or chicken
- ✦ 1 cup fresh bread crumbs
- ✦ 2 tablespoons chopped drained canned pimientos
- ✦ ½ teaspoon celery seed
- ✦ ½ teaspoon salt
- ✦ ⅛ teaspoon white or black pepper
- ✦ ¾ cup low-fat (1% milkfat) milk
- ✦ 2 large egg whites
- ✦ 1 large egg

For the mushroom sauce:
- ✦ 1½ cups sliced fresh mushrooms
- ✦ ½ cup lower-sodium chicken broth (page 67)
- ✦ 1 can (12 ounces) evaporated skimmed milk
- ✦ 3 tablespoons all-purpose flour
- ✦ ⅛ teaspoon of white or black pepper
- ✦ 2 tablespoons minced parsley
- ✦ 1 teaspoon lemon juice

1 To prepare the turkey loaf, preheat the oven to 325°F. In a large mixing bowl, combine the turkey, bread crumbs, pimientos, celery seed, salt, and ⅛ teaspoon pepper. Whisk together the milk, egg whites, and egg. Pour over turkey mixture. Mix thoroughly until combined. Press turkey mixture into a lightly greased 8" x 4" x 2" loaf pan. Bake for 45 to 50 minutes or until loaf is set in center.

2 Meanwhile, to prepare the mushroom sauce, in a medium-size saucepan, combine mushrooms and chicken broth. Bring to a boil. Lower heat and simmer, covered, for 1 minute or until mushrooms are tender.

3 In a small bowl, whisk together the evaporated skimmed milk, flour, and ⅛ teaspoon pepper. Add to mushroom mixture. Cook over moderate heat, whisking constantly, until mixture starts to thicken. Cook and whisk for 2 minutes more or until thickened. Stir in parsley and lemon juice. Serve mushroom sauce over turkey loaf. Make 4 servings.

PREP TIME: **20** MINUTES   COOKING TIME: **45** MINUTES

Turkey Club Sandwich

Turkey Club Sandwich

This appetizing perennial sandwich makes an ideal holiday snack. Some say it was dubbed a club sandwich because it was served in club cars of trains. Others insist it was because the double-decker was a must on country club menus.

- ✦ 4 strips lean bacon, halved
- ✦ 12 slices home-style white or whole-wheat sandwich bread, toasted
- ✦ ½ cup reduced-fat mayonnaise
- ✦ 8 lettuce leaves
- ✦ 1 large tomato, thinly sliced
- ✦ 8 ounces thinly sliced cooked turkey breast
- ✦ 8 tiny sweet pickles (optional)
- ✦ 8 pimiento-stuffed green olives (optional)

1 In a 10-inch skillet, cook bacon over moderate heat until crisp. Drain on paper towels; set aside.

2 Spread one side of each bread slice with some of the mayonnaise. Place a lettuce leaf on the mayonnaise side of 4 bread slices. Top each with some of the sliced tomato and 2 half-strips bacon. Add another slice of bread, mayonnaise side up. Top with remaining lettuce leaves. Divide turkey among sandwiches. Top with remaining bread slices, mayonnaise side down.

3 Cut sandwiches in half diagonally. Thread a pickle and an olive (if using) onto each of 8 wooden picks. Poke a pick into each sandwich half. Makes 4 servings.

PREP TIME: 15 MINUTES COOKING TIME: 5 MINUTES

Turkey Salad Sandwiches

This turkey salad is made the old-fashioned way—by grinding the meat, instead of cutting it into bite-size pieces. This makes the filling easier to spread and less messy to eat.

- ✦ 2 cups ground cooked turkey or chicken
- ✦ 1 can (8 ounces) crushed pineapple packed in juice, drained
- ✦ ¼ cup finely chopped almonds, toasted
- ✦ ¼ cup finely chopped celery
- ✦ ¼ cup reduced-fat mayonnaise
- ✦ 2 tablespoons reduced-fat sour cream
- ✦ 1 teaspoon lemon juice
- ✦ ¼ teaspoon salt
- ✦ 12 slices home-style white or whole-wheat bread
- ✦ 6 lettuce leaves

1 In a medium-size bowl, combine turkey, pineapple, almonds, celery, mayonnaise, sour cream, lemon juice, and salt. Spread the turkey mixture on half of the bread slices. Top with the lettuce leaves and the remaining bread slices. Makes 6 servings.

PREP TIME: 20 MINUTES

Trussing Poultry

 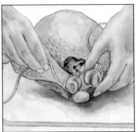

1. Start by spooning some of the stuffing loosely into the neck cavity. Pull the neck skin over the opening and secure it with a small skewer.

2. Next, spoon more stuffing into the body cavity. If there's a band of skin that crosses tail, slip ends of the drumsticks under it. If not, tie drumsticks together with cotton string. Finally, tuck the wing tips under the back.

Roast Goose with Currant Stuffing

A goose gives off more fat during roasting than most other poultry. So have a bulb baster ready to draw off the drippings.

- ✦ 1 large yellow onion, chopped
- ✦ 1 large tart apple, chopped
- ✦ ¼ cup lower-sodium chicken broth (page 67)
- ✦ 6 cups toasted fresh bread crumbs
- ✦ ½ cup currants or chopped raisins
- ✦ ¼ cup slivered almonds, toasted
- ✦ ¼ cup minced parsley
- ✦ 1 teaspoon dried sage leaves
- ✦ ¼ teaspoon each salt and black pepper
- ✦ ⅓ cup lower-sodium chicken broth (page 67)
- ✦ 1 goose (7 to 8 pounds), giblets removed

1 In a small saucepan, combine the onion, apple, and ¼ cup broth. Bring to a boil. Lower heat and simmer for 5 minutes or until onion and apple are tender.

2 In a large mixing bowl, combine onion mixture, bread crumbs, currants, almonds, parsley, sage, salt, and pepper. Toss ⅓ cup broth with bread crumb mixture.

3 Preheat the oven to 350°F. Rinse goose; drain and pat dry. Prick the skin on the lower breast, legs, and around the wings with a skewer. Stuff and truss goose (tip, left). Then, place goose, breast side up, on a rack in large roasting pan. Insert a roasting thermometer in its thigh without touching bone. Spoon remaining stuffing into a lightly greased 1½-quart casserole; cover and refrigerate.

4 Roast goose for 2 to 2½ hours or until the thermometer registers 175°F., draining fat often. Bake the covered casserole of stuffing alongside the goose during the last 30 minutes of roasting. Let the goose stand for 15 to 20 minutes. Carve goose, discarding the skin. Makes 6 servings.

PREP TIME: 20 MINUTES   COOKING TIME: 8 MINUTES
ROASTING TIME: 2 HOURS   STANDING TIME: 15 MINUTES

Danish Fruit-Stuffed Pork Roast

Danish Fruit-Stuffed Pork Roast

This apple-and-prune-stuffed roast is traditionally served at Christmas in Danish families. For an extra-special touch, try making the stuffing with raisin bread.

+ 1 pork loin center rib roast (4 pounds), backbone loosened
+ ⅛ teaspoon each salt and black pepper

For the stuffing:
+ 1 cup pitted prunes
+ ⅔ cup water
+ 3 tablespoons butter or margarine
+ 1 small yellow onion, chopped
+ 2 tablespoons firmly packed light brown sugar
+ 1 teaspoon grated lemon rind

+ ½ teaspoon ground cinnamon
+ ¼ teaspoon ground cardamom
+ 6 cups dried bread cubes
+ 1 large tart apple, chopped
+ ½ cup apple juice

1 Preheat the oven to 325°F. Place the roast rib side down. Using a sharp knife, cut deep slits between the rib bones of the roast. Cut through the thickest portion of the meat about halfway to the backbone and within ½ inch of the edges to make each pocket. Sprinkle the roast with the salt and pepper.

2 To prepare the stuffing, in a small saucepan, combine the prunes and the water. Bring to a boil. Lower the heat and simmer, covered, until prunes are

tender. Drain. Coarsely chop prunes; set aside.

3 In the same saucepan, melt the butter over moderate heat. Add the onion and cook for 3 minutes or until tender. Remove from heat. Stir in the brown sugar, lemon rind, cinnamon, and cardamom.

4 Place the bread cubes in a large bowl. Stir in the onion mixture, prunes, and apple. Drizzle with the apple juice, tossing lightly until moistened. Spoon about 3 tablespoons of the stuffing into each pocket of roast. Spoon the remaining stuffing into a 1½-quart casserole; cover and refrigerate.

5 Place the roast, rib side down, in a roasting pan. Roast for 1¾ to 2¼ hours or until an instant-read thermometer inserted in the center of roast (not stuffing) registers 155°F. (Cover the roast loosely with foil after 1 hour so the stuffing doesn't overbrown.) Bake the covered casserole of stuffing alongside the roast during the last 30 to 40 minutes of roasting.

6 Let the roast stand for 15 minutes before carving. Serve the stuffing in the casserole with the roast. Makes 8 servings.
PREP TIME: 35 MINUTES COOKING TIME: 2 HOURS
5 MINUTES STANDING TIME: 15 MINUTES

Country Pork Loin Roast with Cherry Sauce

In the old days, hogs were often called "mortgage lifters" because, unlike grain crops, farmers could rely on them for their income in any weather. Farm women created special recipes to use the abundance of pork.

- ✦ 1 boneless pork single-loin roast
    (3 to 3½ pounds), trimmed
- ✦ 1⅛ teaspoon each salt and black pepper
For the sauce:
- ✦ 4 teaspoons cornstarch
- ✦ ¼ teaspoon ground coriander
- ✦ ⅛ teaspoon ground nutmeg
- ✦ 1 cup cranberry juice cocktail
- ✦ ½ cup red currant jelly
- ✦ 2 cups frozen and thawed pitted tart red
    cherries, drained, or 1 can (16 ounces)
    pitted tart red cherries, drained

1 Preheat the oven to 325°F. Sprinkle the meat with the salt and pepper, then place it on a rack in a roasting pan. Insert a roasting thermometer in the center. Roast for 1¼ to 1¾ hours or until thermometer registers 155°F. Cover the meat with foil and let stand for 15 minutes before carving.

2 Meanwhile, to prepare the sauce, in a medium-size saucepan, combine the cornstarch, coriander, and nutmeg. Stir in the cranberry juice cocktail and jelly.

3 Cook over moderate heat, whisking constantly, until mixture starts to thicken. Cook for 2 minutes more or until the mixture is thickened, whisking constantly. Stir in the cherries and cook until heated through. Serve the sauce with the meat and hot cooked rice. Makes 8 to 10 servings.
PREP TIME: 10 MINUTES COOKING TIME: 1¼ HOURS
STANDING TIME: 15 MINUTES

Sage Roast Pork

This hearty dish gets its robust flavor from garlic cloves stuffed into slits in the meat and a sprinkling of dried sage and thyme.

- ✦ 1 boneless pork double-loin roast
    (3 pounds), trimmed and tied
- ✦ 2 large cloves of garlic, cut into slivers
- ✦ 1 tablespoon olive or vegetable oil
- ✦ 1½ teaspoons each dried sage leaves and
    thyme leaves
- ✦ ½ teaspoon salt
- ✦ ¼ teaspoon freshly ground black pepper
- ✦ ½ cup dry white wine or lower-sodium
    chicken broth (page 67)
- ✦ 2 tablespoons minced parsley

1 Preheat the oven to 325°F. Cut about 12 small slits randomly around the meat. Insert the garlic slivers into the slits. Rub the surface of the meat with the oil. Sprinkle with the sage, thyme, salt, and pepper. Rub into the meat.

2 Place the meat on a rack in a roasting pan. Use a pan made from heavy gauge metal that is designed to take the heat of a range-top burner.

3 Insert a roasting thermometer in the center. Roast, uncovered, for 1¾ to 2 hours or until thermometer registers 155°F. Transfer the meat to a platter. Cover the meat with foil and let stand for 15 minutes before carving.

4 Meanwhile, pour the wine into the roasting pan, stirring to loosen the browned bits. Cook over moderate heat on the top of the range until the mixture starts to bubble. Cook until slightly thickened.

5 Slice meat; drizzle wine mixture over meat. Sprinkle with the parsley. Makes 8 servings.
PREP TIME: 10 MINUTES COOKING TIME: 1 HOUR
50 MINUTES STANDING TIME: 15 MINUTES

Maple-Glazed Ham with Raisin Sauce

In bygone days, country women saved ham for festive occasions and then served it with raisin sauce.

- ✦ 1 cooked ham, shank portion (4 to 4½ pounds)
- ✦ 2 tablespoons whole cloves

For the maple glaze:
- ✦ ¼ cup maple-flavored syrup or maple syrup
- ✦ 1 tablespoon butter or margarine
- ✦ 1 tablespoon light corn syrup
- ✦ 1 tablespoon orange juice
- ✦ ⅛ teaspoon ground allspice
- ✦ Dash ground cloves

For the raisin sauce:
- ✦ ¼ cup firmly packed light brown sugar
- ✦ 2 tablespoons cornstarch
- ✦ 1½ cups apple juice
- ✦ 1 cup raisins
- ✦ 3 tablespoons orange juice
- ✦ 1 tablespoon vinegar
- ✦ 1 teaspoon grated orange rind
- ✦ ⅛ teaspoon ground allspice

1 Preheat the oven to 325°F. Score the top of the ham into diamonds, then stud the ham with whole cloves (tip, right). Place the ham on a rack in a large shallow baking pan. Insert a roasting thermometer in the center of the thickest portion without touching bone. Bake for 1¼ hours.

2 Meanwhile, to prepare the maple glaze, in a small saucepan, combine the maple-flavored syrup, butter, corn syrup, the 1 tablespoon orange juice, ⅛ teaspoon allspice, and ground cloves. Bring to a boil; remove the pan from heat.

3 Brush the ham with some of the maple glaze. Bake for 15 minutes more or until thermometer registers 135°F., brushing once or twice with the remaining glaze. Cover ham with foil and let stand for 15 minutes before carving.

4 Meanwhile, to prepare the raisin sauce, in a medium-size saucepan, combine the brown sugar and cornstarch. Stir in the apple juice, raisins, the 3 tablespoons orange juice, vinegar, orange rind, and ⅛ teaspoon allspice.

5 Cook over moderate heat, stirring constantly, until the mixture starts to thicken. Cook and stir for 1 to 2 minutes more or until thickened. Serve the ham with the raisin sauce. Makes 10 servings.

PREP TIME: 15 MINUTES COOKING TIME: 1½ HOURS
STANDING TIME: 15 MINUTES

Scoring Ham

Add an old-fashioned, decorative touch to baked ham by scoring the top and studding it with cloves. The scoring also allows the glaze to penetrate the meat.

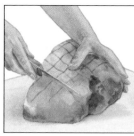 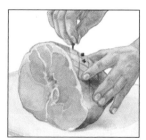

1. To score the ham, use a small sharp knife to diagonally cut ¼-inch-deep parallel lines in the top of the ham about 1 inch apart. Make another series of cuts at right angles to form diamonds.

2. Using your fingers, insert a whole clove in the middle of each of the diamonds. You may find it easier to pierce the meat first with the point of a skewer and then insert the clove.

Maple-Glazed Ham with Apricot-Berry Sauce

Prepare as for Maple-Glazed Ham with Raisin Sauce, omitting the ingredients for the raisin sauce. To prepare the apricot-berry sauce, in a medium-size saucepan, combine ¼ cup firmly packed light brown sugar and 2 tablespoons cornstarch. Stir in 1½ cups orange juice. Cook over moderate heat, stirring constantly, until mixture starts to thicken. Cook and stir for 1 to 2 minutes or until thickened. Stir in 1 can (16 ounces) unpeeled apricot halves packed in light syrup, drained and sliced; heat through. Stir in 1½ cups sliced strawberries.

Ham with Plum Sauce

Many old-time recipes combined ham with fruits. If you can't find ripe plums for this recipe, use a large tart red apple instead.

- ✦ 1 cooked center-cut ham slice (1½ pounds), 1 inch thick and trimmed
- ✦ 1 tablespoon butter or margarine

- 2 tablespoons firmly packed light brown sugar
- ¾ teaspoon dry mustard
- ½ teaspoon ground nutmeg
- ⅛ teaspoon ground cloves
- 1 can (15¼ ounces) pineapple slices packed in juice
- Orange juice
- 3 medium-size plums, sliced, or 1 large tart red apple, cored and thinly sliced
- ⅓ cup dry sherry or orange juice
- 2 tablespoons cornstarch

1 Slash the edge of the ham slice at 1-inch intervals. In a 12-inch skillet, melt the butter over moderate heat. Stir in the brown sugar, mustard, nutmeg, and cloves. Add the ham to the skillet and cook for 5 minutes on each side or until ham is browned.

2 Drain the pineapple, reserving the juice. Set aside the pineapple slices. Add enough orange juice to the pineapple juice to measure 1 cup liquid. Pour the pineapple liquid over ham. Bring to a boil. Lower the heat and simmer, covered, for 10 minutes. Add the pineapple slices and plums. Simmer, covered, for 5 minutes more or until ham is heated through. Transfer the ham to a platter; cover with foil and keep warm.

3 In a small bowl, stir together the sherry and cornstarch, then stir into the fruit mixture. Cook for 2 minutes or until the mixture thickens. Serve the fruit mixture over ham. Makes 6 servings.

PREP TIME: 15 MINUTES COOKING TIME: 25 MINUTES

Baked Ham Slice with Cranberry-Honey Sauce

The center-cut ham slice is not a modern convenience— it dates back to pioneer times, when it was often served with cranberries.

- 1 cooked center-cut ham slice (1½ pounds), 1 inch thick and trimmed
- 1 tablespoon whole cloves
- ½ cup dry red wine or orange juice
- ¼ cup honey
- ½ teaspoon ground ginger
- ¼ teaspoon ground allspice
- 1½ cups cranberries
- 1 cup frozen small whole onions

1 Preheat the oven to 350°F. Score the top of the ham slice into diamonds; stud the ham with the cloves (tip, opposite page). Slash the edge of ham at 1-inch intervals. Place the ham on a rack in a shallow backing pan. Bake for 30 minutes or until heated through.

2 Meanwhile, in a medium-size saucepan, combine the wine, honey, ginger, and allspice. Bring to a boil. Stir in the cranberries and onions. Return to a boil. Boil gently over moderately high heat for 5 minutes or until the cranberry skins pop. Serve the cranberry mixture over the ham. Makes 6 servings.

PREP TIME: 10 MINUTES COOKING TIME: 30 MINUTES

To add variety to your holiday dinner table, serve ham with a flavorful fruit sauce.

Holiday Beverages

Orange Eggnog Punch (top right), Hospitality Punch (bottom right), and Buttered Rum Toddy (left)

Orange Eggnog Punch

This traditional holiday beverage gets fresh sparkle and flavor from the addition of ginger ale and orange juice.

- ✦ 1 quart reduced-fat dairy eggnog or 1 can (1 quart) eggnog
- ✦ 1 can (12 ounces) frozen orange juice concentrate, thawed
- ✦ 1 can (12 ounces) ginger ale, chilled

1 In a pitcher, stir eggnog and orange juice concentrate until well mixed. Pour in ginger ale and stir gently. Makes eight 7-ounce servings.
PREP TIME: 5 MINUTES

Hot Cinnamon Cider

At Christmas, serve this memorable hot cider in big mugs. Always just simmer the cider, never boil it.

- ✦ 4 cups (1 quart) apple cider
- ✦ 1 cup orange juice
- ✦ 2 tablespoons honey
- ✦ 12 whole allspice berries
- ✦ 4 cinnamon sticks, each 3 inches long
- ✦ 1 whole nutmeg
- ✦ ½ teaspoon grated orange rind
- ✦ 1 small red apple, cored and cut into wedges

1 In a medium-size saucepan, bring the cider, orange juice, honey, allspice berries, cinnamon sticks, whole nutmeg, and orange rind to a boil over high heat. Lower the heat and simmer, uncovered, for 10 minutes. Add apple wedges and simmer for 3 minutes more.

2 Remove from heat. Strain into a heat-proof pitcher, reserving apple wedges. To serve, place a few of the apple wedges in each cup and fill cups with cider. Makes four 7-ounce servings.

PREP TIME: 5 MINUTES COOKING TIME: 18 MINUTES

Buttered Rum Toddy

Pioneers made potent toddies to chase the chills away. This milder version has the same flavor but less alcohol.

- ◆ 1¼ cups water
- ◆ ¼ cup honey
- ◆ 3 tablespoons lemon juice
- ◆ ½ cup dark rum
- ◆ Butter or vanilla ice cream
- ◆ Ground nutmeg

1 In a medium-size saucepan, heat the water, honey, and lemon juice over moderate heat until heated through. Remove from heat and stir in the rum.

2 Pour the rum mixture into mugs. Float a small pat of butter or a tiny scoop of ice cream on each toddy. Sprinkle nutmeg over the butter or ice cream. Makes two 8-ounce servings.

PREP TIME: 5 MINUTES COOKING TIME: 5 MINUTES

Hospitality Punch

Punches made with tea and fruit juice were popular in the 1930's and 1940's. Some cookbooks contained detailed recipes, while others just instructed readers to add brewed tea to a fruit punch.

- ◆ 2 cups hot brewed tea
- ◆ ½ cup sugar
- ◆ 2 cups unsweetened pineapple juice
- ◆ 1 cup orange juice
- ◆ ½ cup lemon juice
- ◆ 3 cups chilled ginger ale

1 In a heat-proof pitcher, pour the tea over the sugar and stir until the sugar dissolves. Add the pineapple juice, orange juice, and lemon juice. Cover and refrigerate at least 4 hours (will keep for 1 day). To serve, pour the tea mixture into a small punch bowl and pour in the ginger ale. Makes twelve 6-ounce servings.

PREP TIME: 10 MINUTES CHILLING TIME: 4 HOURS

Two Favorite Party Dips

Guacamole

Its buttery consistency and Mexican flavors (fresh cilantro and hot chilies) make this a popular dip.

- ◆ 2 large, very ripe avocados
- ◆ ¼ cup freshly squeezed lime juice
- ◆ 1 large ripe tomato, finely chopped and drained
- ◆ 2 tablespoons cilantro, freshly chopped
- ◆ 3 tablespoons red onion, finely chopped
- ◆ 1 tablespoon extra virgin olive oil

1 Cut the avocados in half and remove the stone. Scoop out the avocado flesh from the skin, place in a small bowl, and cover immediately with the lime juice. Mash the avocado and lime juice together with the back of a spoon until the avocado has an even, rough-textured consistency.

2 Gently blend the tomato pieces and all remaining ingredients into the mashed avocado.

3 Cover the bowl tightly with plastic wrap and refrigerate the guacamole until about a half hour before it is needed. Leave, covered, outside the refrigerator to come to room temperature before serving. Garnish with a chopped chili or a few cilantro leaves. Makes about 2 cups.

TOTAL TIME: 15 MINUTES

Tzatziki

This easy-to-make Greek dish flavored with garlic and cucumber can be used as a dip or as a spread.

- ◆ 1 medium cucumber, peeled
- ◆ 2 cups yogurt
- ◆ 1 clove garlic, finely chopped
- ◆ 1 tablespoon mint, freshly chopped
- ◆ 2 tablespoons olive oil
- ◆ kosher salt and freshly ground
- ◆ black pepper

1 Dice the cucumber and dry the pieces well between sheets of paper towel.

2 Stir the cucumber into the yogurt, add the remaining ingredients, and season to taste with kosher salt and freshly ground pepper.

3 Place the tzatziki in a bowl and drizzle olive oil over the top. Makes about 2 cups.

TOTAL TIME: 10 MINUTES

⚓ *Delicious Side Dishes* ⚓

German Red Cabbage

To keep red cabbage an attractive rosy color, always cook it with something acidic, like cider vinegar or lemon juice.

- ◆ 1 tablespoon olive or vegetable oil
- ◆ 5 cups coarsely shredded red cabbage
- ◆ ¼ cup apple or currant jelly
- ◆ ¼ cup dry red wine or lower-sodium chicken broth (page 67)
- ◆ 4 teaspoons cider vinegar
- ◆ ⅛ teaspoon each salt and black pepper
- ◆ ⅛ teaspoon ground cloves
- ◆ 2 medium-size apples, cored and cut into 1-inch chunks
- ◆ 1 tablespoon all-purpose flour

1 In a 12-inch skillet, heat the oil over moderate heat. Add the cabbage and cook for 5 minutes. Stir in the apple jelly, 2 tablespoons of the red wine, the vinegar, salt, pepper, and cloves. Stir in apples. Bring to a boil. Lower the heat and simmer, covered, for 10 minutes or until the cabbage is crisp-tender, stirring frequently.

2 In a small bowl, stir together the remaining 2 tablespoons red wine and the flour, then stir into cabbage mixture. Cook over moderate heat, stirring constantly, until mixture starts to thicken. Cook and stir for 2 minutes more or until thickened. Makes 4 servings.

PREP TIME: 15 MINUTES COOKING TIME: 25 MINUTES

Orange-Raisin Carrots

This easy-to-make mixture makes a refreshing addition to your holiday table.

- ◆ 8 medium-size carrots, sliced
- ◆ ⅓ cup raisins
- ◆ ⅓ cup orange juice
- ◆ 1 tablespoon firmly packed light brown sugar
- ◆ 1 teaspoon cornstarch
- ◆ ½ teaspoon grated orange rind
- ◆ ¼ teaspoon ground ginger

1 In a large saucepan, bring ½ inch of water to a boil over high heat. Add the carrots. Lower the heat

and simmer, covered, for 7 to 9 minutes or until carrots are crisp-tender. Drain.

2 Meanwhile, in a small saucepan, stir together the raisins, orange juice, brown sugar, cornstarch, orange rind, and ginger. Bring to a boil over moderate heat, stirring constantly. Cook for 2 minutes or until mixture is thickened, stirring constantly.

3 Pour over the carrots; toss until mixed. Serve with grilled or broiled burgers. Makes 4 servings.
PREP TIME: 15 MINUTES COOKING TIME: 12 MINUTES

Nan's Circles and Squares

This old-timey medley of carrots, sweet pepper, and green olives goes well with any simple main dish, such as grilled chicken, steak, or fish.

- ◆ 1 tablespoon butter or margarine
- ◆ 1 large yellow onion, sliced
- ◆ 1 medium-size sweet red or green pepper, chopped
- ◆ 6 medium-size carrots, sliced
- ◆ ½ cup apple juice
- ◆ 1 teaspoon dried basil leaves
- ◆ ¼ teaspoon salt
- ◆ ⅛ teaspoon black pepper
- ◆ 1 teaspoon cornstarch
- ◆ 2 tablespoons cut-up pimiento-stuffed green olives
- ◆ 1 tablespoon minced parsley

1 In a large saucepan, melt the butter over moderate heat. Add the onion and red pepper and cook for 5 minutes or until vegetables are tender. Stir in carrots, ¼ cup of the apple juice, basil, salt, and black pepper.

2 Bring to a boil. Lower the heat and simmer, covered, for 7 to 9 minutes or until carrots are crisp-tender.

3 In a small bowl, stir together the remaining ¼ cup apple juice and the cornstarch, then stir into the simmering carrot mixture. Cook for 2 minutes or until mixture is thickened. Remove from heat. Stir in the olives. Sprinkle with parsley. Makes 4 servings.
PREP TIME: 15 MINUTES COOKING TIME: 20 MINUTES

Fancy-Fixin's Cauliflower

Fancy-Fixin's Cauliflower

In Pudd'nhead Wilson's Calendar, Mark Twain proclaims, "Cauliflower is nothing but cabbage with a college education." This zesty recipe dresses up the "educated" vegetable with a tangy sauce.

- ✦ 1 small head cauliflower or 3 cups frozen cauliflower
- ✦ 1 tablespoon olive or vegetable oil
- ✦ 1 stalk celery, thinly sliced
- ✦ 2 tablespoons cider vinegar
- ✦ 2 tablespoons lower-sodium chicken broth (page 67) or water
- ✦ 1 tablespoon chopped drained canned pimientos
- ✦ 1 teaspoon sugar
- ✦ ¼ teaspoon dried thyme leaves
- ✦ ⅛ teaspoon black pepper

1 Cut fresh cauliflower into flowerets. In a large saucepan, bring ½ inch of lightly salted water to a boil over high heat. Add the cauliflower. Lower the heat and simmer, covered, for 8 to 10 minutes or until crisp-tender. (Or, cook the frozen cauliflower according to package directions.) Drain; transfer cauliflower to a serving bowl.

2 Meanwhile, in a small saucepan, heat the oil over moderate heat. Add the celery and cook for 5 minutes or until tender. Stir in the vinegar, chicken broth, pimientos, sugar, thyme, and pepper. Drizzle over the cauliflower and toss until mixed. Makes 4 servings.

PREP TIME: 10 MINUTES   COOKING TIME: 13 MINUTES

Tomato and Cucumber Aspic

In the old days, cool aspics usually were served in the summer when tomatoes were ripe. Today, you can enjoy this zesty salad at holiday time because it's made with hot-style vegetable juice cocktail.

- ✦ 1 envelope unflavored gelatin (2 teaspoons)
- ✦ 3 cans (5½ ounces each) hot-style vegetable juice cocktail
- ✦ 1 teaspoon lower-sodium Worcestershire sauce
- ✦ ⅛ teaspoon hot red pepper sauce (optional)
- ✦ 1 teaspoon dried dill weed
- ✦ ½ teaspoon grated lemon rind
- ✦ Nonstick cooking spray
- ✦ ½ cup seeded and finely chopped cucumber
- ✦ ¼ cup finely chopped sweet green, red, or yellow pepper
- ✦ 2 large green onions with tops, finely sliced

1 In a medium-size bowl, sprinkle the gelatin over 1 can of the vegetable juice; let stand for 1 minute. In a medium-size saucepan, bring the remaining vegetable juice, Worcestershire sauce, and red pepper sauce (if using) to a boil. Add to gelatin; stir until gelatin dissolves completely. Stir in the dill weed and lemon rind. Cover gelatin mixture with plastic wrap; refrigerate for 2½ hours or until thickened but not solid (a spoon will leave an impression when drawn through it).

2 Coat a 3½-cup mold with cooking spray. Fold the cucumber, green pepper, and green onions into juice mixture. Spoon into mold. Cover and refrigerate for 2½ hours more or until firm.

3 To serve, unmold salad onto plate. Tuck leaf lettuce around base of salad. Makes 6 side-dish servings.
PREP TIME: 15 MINUTES COOKING TIME: 5 MINUTES
CHILLING TIME: 5 HOURS

Cranberry Pecan Mold

Handsome, shimmering gelatin molds were the traditional accompaniment to holiday roasted turkey. This recipe also goes well with roasted chicken or pork.

- ✦ 1 can (11 ounces) mandarin orange sections
- ✦ Orange juice
- ✦ 1 package (3 ounces) cherry-flavored gelatin mix
- ✦ ½ cup cranberry-orange or cranberry-raspberry sauce (recipe, below)
- ✦ Nonstick cooking spray
- ✦ ½ cup finely chopped Granny Smith apple
- ✦ ¼ cup chopped pecans or walnuts, toasted

1 Drain orange sections, reserving syrup. Add enough orange juice to syrup to measure 1¼ cups liquid. In a medium-size saucepan, bring the orange juice mixture to a boil. Remove from heat. Add gelatin to hot mixture; stir until gelatin dissolves. In a medium-size bowl, combine gelatin mixture and cranberry-orange sauce.

2 Cover gelatin mixture with plastic wrap; refrigerate for 2½ hours or until thickened but not solid (a spoon will leave an impression when drawn through it).

3 Coat a 3½-cup mold with cooking spray. Fold the mandarin oranges, apple, and nuts into gelatin mixture. Spoon into mold. Cover and refrigerate for 2½ hours more or until firm.

4 To serve, unmold the salad onto a plate. Tuck red-tipped leaf lettuce around base of salad. Makes 6 side-dish servings.
PREP TIME: 10 MINUTES COOKING TIME: 5 MINUTES
CHILLING TIME: 5 HOURS

Cranberry-Raspberry Sauce

In a large saucepan, put **1 package (12 ounces) of fresh or frozen cranberries, 2 cups of fresh or frozen raspberries, 1 cup Merlot red wine, and ¾ cup sugar.** Bring to a boil, stirring occasionally. Use a whisk to mask the cranberries. Lower heat and let simmer for 15 minutes. Pour the sauce into a container and refrigerate. Serve hot or cold. Makes about 4½ cups.

Unmolding Salads

Coaxing a gelatin salad out of its mold is easy if you know these simple tricks.

1 Dip the mold in warm water for a few seconds.

2 Loosen the salad edges with the tip of a knife.

3 Invert a serving plate over the mold. While grasping the plate tightly against the mold, quickly flip both over. Shake gently until the salad slides out of the mold.

Cranberry Pecan Mold

Orange-Glazed Beets and Broccoli Polonaise

Orange-Glazed Beets

Old-time cookbooks advise cooking whole beets with the stem end left on so they don't "bleed" while they're cooking.

- ✦ 1¼ pounds fresh beets or 2 cans (16 ounces each) diced beets, drained
- ✦ ⅓ cup lower-calorie orange marmalade
- ✦ 1 tablespoon cornstarch
- ✦ 1 tablespoon honey
- ✦ 1 tablespoon cider vinegar
- ✦ ⅛ teaspoon ground cinnamon
- ✦ Dash ground allspice

1 Trim fresh beets ½ inch above the stems. In a large saucepan, cover the beets with lightly salted water. Bring to a boil over high heat. Lower the heat and simmer, covered, for 40 to 45 minutes or until almost tender. Drain, removing the beets. Cool slightly. Peel by slipping off skins while still warm; cut into ½-inch cubes. (Or, use canned diced beets.)

2 In the same saucepan, stir together the marmalade, cornstarch, honey, vinegar, cinnamon, and allspice. Bring to a boil over moderate heat, stirring constantly.

3 Stir in the beets. Cook for 3 to 4 minutes or until beets are heated through, stirring occasionally. Makes 4 servings.

PREP TIME: 20 MINUTES COOKING TIME: 55 MINUTES

Broccoli Polonaise

Vegetables served polonaise-style are topped with a mixture of butter, bread crumbs, parsley, and hard-cooked egg. You also can serve this topping over steamed asparagus or cauliflower.

- ✦ 1 pound fresh broccoli spears or 1 package (16 ounces) frozen broccoli spears
- ✦ 1 tablespoon butter or margarine
- ✦ ⅓ cup seasoned fine dry bread crumbs
- ✦ 2 tablespoons minced parsley
- ✦ ½ teaspoon grated lemon rind
- ✦ ⅛ teaspoon ground red pepper (cayenne)
- ✦ 1 hard-cooked large egg, finely chopped

1 In a large saucepan, bring ½ inch of water to a boil over high heat. Add the fresh broccoli. Lower the heat and simmer, covered, for 8 to 10 minutes or until crisp-tender. (Or, cook the frozen broccoli according to package directions.) Drain and arrange the broccoli on a platter.

2 Meanwhile, in a small saucepan, heat the butter over moderate heat until lightly browned. Stir in the bread crumbs, parsley, lemon rind, ground red pepper, and hard-cooked egg. Spoon over the cooked broccoli. Makes 4 servings.

PREP TIME: 10 MINUTES COOKING TIME: 13 MINUTES

Glazed Onions

Onions were one of the first crops the colonists planted when they came to North America. This old recipe features onions cooked in a buttery, sweet, golden glaze.

- ✦ 3 large yellow onions, sliced and separated into rings
- ✦ 2 tablespoons butter or margarine
- ✦ 2 tablespoons sugar
- ✦ ¼ teaspoon ground ginger
- ✦ Dash salt

1 In a large saucepan, bring ½ inch of water to a boil over high heat. Add the onions. Lower the heat and simmer, covered, for 10 minutes or until tender. Drain.

2 Meanwhile, in a 10-inch skillet, melt the butter over moderate heat. Stir in the sugar, ginger, and salt until sugar is dissolved. Add the onions. Cook, uncovered, for 2 to 3 minutes or until onions are glazed and most of the liquid has evaporated, stirring frequently. Makes 4 servings.

PREP TIME: 10 MINUTES COOKING TIME: 17 MINUTES

Glazed Carrots

Prepare as for Glazed Onions, substituting **8 medium-size carrots,** sliced, for the onions and ¼ **teaspoon dried mint leaves** for the ginger. Cook the carrots in water for 7 to 9 minutes or until tender, then continue as directed in step 2 of Glazed Onions.

Glazed Parsnips

Prepare as for Glazed Onions, substituting **6 medium-size parsnips, sliced,** for the onions and **2 tablespoons firmly packed light brown sugar** for the sugar. Cook parsnips in water for 7 to 9 minutes or until tender, then continue as directed in step 2 of Glazed Onions.

Gran's Potato Pancakes

When you make these old-time pancakes, be sure to turn them carefully so that the tasty brown crust won't stick to the skillet.

+ 6 medium-size potatoes
  (about 2 pounds total)
+ ¼ cup low-fat (1% milkfat) milk
+ 1 tablespoon butter or margarine
+ ½ teaspoon salt
+ ¼ teaspoon paprika
+ ¼ teaspoon black pepper
+ 4 medium-size green onions with tops,
  finely chopped
+ 2 large egg whites, lightly beaten
+ Nonstick cooking spray
+ 1 tablespoon vegetable oil

1 Peel and quarter potatoes. In a large saucepan, cover the potatoes with water. Bring to a boil over high heat. Lower the heat and simmer, covered, for 20 to 25 minutes or until tender. Drain.

2 In a medium-size bowl, with the electric mixer on *Low*, beat potatoes until almost smooth. Add milk, butter, salt, paprika, and pepper. Beat until light and fluffy. Cover and refrigerate for at least 1 hour.

3 Stir the green onions and egg whites into potato mixture until well mixed. Coat a 10-inch nonstick skillet with cooking spray. Add the oil to skillet. Heat the oil over moderate heat.

4 Spoon half of the potato mixture into 4 mounds in the skillet; flatten tops slightly. Cook for 4 to 5 minutes on each side or until browned, turning carefully. Cover and keep warm. Repeat with remaining potato mixture, adding more oil if necessary. Makes 4 servings.
PREP TIME: 15 MINUTES CHILLING TIME: 1 HOUR COOKING TIME: 47 MINUTES

Potatoes Lyonnaise

This old-fashioned recipe called for lots of butter. To reduce the fat, this version uses a small amount of olive oil instead.

+ 3 medium-size potatoes (about 1 pound
  total), thinly sliced
+ 1 medium-size yellow onion, thinly sliced
  and separated into rings
+ 1 tablespoon olive or vegetable oil
+ ½ teaspoon salt

+ ¼ teaspoon black pepper
+ 2 tablespoons minced parsley

1 Preheat the oven to 425°F. In a medium-size saucepan, cover the potatoes with water. Bring to a boil over high heat. Lower the heat and simmer, covered, for 12 to 15 minutes or until potatoes are almost tender. Drain well; pat dry with paper towels.

2 Spread the potatoes and onion in a lightly greased 15½" x 10½" x 1" baking pan. Drizzle with the oil. Sprinkle with the salt and pepper. Bake, covered, for 15 minutes or until onion is tender. Bake, uncovered, for 15 to 20 minutes more or until potatoes and onion are browned. Sprinkle with parsley. Makes 3 servings.
PREP TIME: 15 MINUTES COOKING TIME: 52 MINUTES

Sweet Potato Pecan Casserole

For this recipe, select sweet potatoes with deep orange skin and meat. They are moist and great for mashing. The tan-skinned sweet potatoes have yellow flesh, a drier texture, and are better for baking.

+ 4 medium-size sweet potatoes
  (about 2 pounds total)
+ 2 large egg whites
+ 2 tablespoons honey or firmly packed
  light brown sugar
+ 1 tablespoon butter or margarine
+ ¼ teaspoon salt
+ ⅛ teaspoon ground nutmeg
+ 2 tablespoons finely chopped pecans

1 Peel and quarter sweet potatoes. In a large saucepan, cover the sweet potatoes with water. Bring to a boil over high heat. Lower the heat and simmer, covered, for 20 to 25 minutes or until tender. Drain.

2 Preheat the oven to 350°F. In a large bowl, with an electric mixer on *Low*, beat the potatoes until almost smooth. Add the egg whites, honey, butter, salt, and nutmeg. Beat until light and fluffy.

3 Spoon the sweet potato mixture into an 8-inch round baking pan. Sprinkle with pecans. Bake for 25 minutes or until heated through. Makes 4 servings.
PREP TIME: 15 MINUTES COOKING TIME: 55 MINUTES

Old-Time Scalloped Potatoes

Old-Time Scalloped Potatoes

Enhance hearty holiday meals with these stick-to-the-ribs potatoes, which are baked in a creamy sauce and topped with cheese.

- ✦ 4 medium-size potatoes (about 1⅓ pounds total), peeled and thinly sliced
- ✦ 1 medium-size yellow onion, chopped
- ✦ ¼ cup water
- ✦ ¼ teaspoon each salt and black pepper
- ✦ ¼ teaspoon celery seeds (optional)
- ✦ 1½ cups low-fat (1% milkfat) milk
- ✦ 3 tablespoons all-purpose flour
- ✦ 2 tablespoons minced parsley
- ✦ ½ cup shredded reduced-fat Cheddar cheese (2 ounces)

1 In a large saucepan, cover the potatoes with water. Bring to a boil over high heat. Lower the heat and simmer, covered, for 12 to 15 minutes or until potatoes are almost tender. Drain.

2 Preheat the oven to 350°F. Meanwhile, in a small saucepan, combine the onion and the ¼ cup water. Bring to a boil. Lower the heat and simmer, covered, for 5 minutes or until tender. Drain. Stir in the salt, pepper, and celery seeds (if using). In a small bowl, whisk together the milk and flour. Stir into the onion mixture. Cook over moderate heat, stirring constantly, until mixture starts to thicken. Cook and stir for 2 minutes or until thickened. Stir in the parsley.

3 Place half of the potatoes in a lightly greased 1½-quart casserole. Cover with half of the milk mixture. Add the remaining potatoes and remaining milk mixture. Bake for 20 minutes or until heated through. Sprinkle with the Cheddar. Makes 4 servings.

PREP TIME: 20 MINUTES COOKING TIME: 42 MINUTES

Sweets and Treats

Christmas Plum Pudding With Brandied Cider Sauce

Christmas Plum Pudding with Brandied Cider Sauce

Although often confused with fruitcake, this classic Christmas dessert tastes more like a rich, dense spice cake. This version uses butter instead of the traditional suet and can be made with your choice of candied fruit, currants, or raisins.

- ✦ 1¼ cups all-purpose flour
- ✦ 1 teaspoon grated orange rind
- ✦ 1 teaspoon ground cinnamon
- ✦ ¾ teaspoon baking powder
- ✦ ½ teaspoon ground ginger
- ✦ ⅛ teaspoon ground cloves

- ✦ ½ cup firmly packed light brown sugar
- ✦ ¼ cup butter or margarine, at room temperature
- ✦ 4 large egg whites
- ✦ ½ cup apple cider or apple juice
- ✦ ¾ cup raisins
- ✦ ½ cup shredded carrot
- ✦ ⅓ cup candied cherries, halved, or currants or raisins
- ✦ ⅓ cup chopped candied pineapple, currants, or raisins
- ✦ ⅓ cup pecan halves
- ✦ Brandied Cider Sauce (recipe, opposite)

1 Lightly grease a 1½-quart steamed pudding mold or casserole. In a medium-size bowl, stir together the flour, orange rind, cinnamon, baking powder, ginger, and cloves.

2 In a large bowl, with an electric mixer on *Medium*, cream the brown sugar and butter until light and fluffy, scraping side of bowl often. Add the egg whites and beat well. Using a wooden spoon, stir in one-third of the flour mixture, then half of the apple cider. Repeat, then stir in the remaining flour mixture. Stir in the raisins, carrot, cherries, pineapple, and pecans.

3 Spoon the batter evenly into the prepared mold. Cover mold with foil. Tie foil in place with string.

4 Place mold on a rack in a Dutch oven. Pour boiling water into the Dutch oven until the water is halfway up the side of the mold.

5 Cook, covered, over low heat for 2 to 2½ hours or until a toothpick inserted in the center comes out clean.

6 Place mold upright on a wire rack and let stand for 10 minutes.

7 Using a narrow metal spatula, loosen side of plum pudding from the mold, then invert the pudding onto a serving plate.

8 Serve warm with Brandied Cider Sauce; top with vanilla ice cream if you like. (Or, cover and refrigerate the pudding—will keep for 1 week. To reheat the pudding, steam as directed in step 4 for 1 hour or until heated through.) Makes 8 servings.

PREP TIME: 25 MINUTES
COOKING TIME: 2 HOURS
STANDING TIME: 10 MINUTES

Brandied Cider Sauce

In a small saucepan, whisk together ¾ cup apple cider or apple juice, ¼ cup firmly packed light brown sugar, and 1 tablespoon cornstarch. Bring to a boil over moderate heat, whisking constantly. Cook for 2 minutes or until the mixture is thickened, whisking constantly. Stir in 2 tablespoons brandy or apple juice and 1 teaspoon butter or margarine. Makes about ¾ cup.

Traditional Christmas Cake

This rich cake can be made at the last minute before Christmas—it doesn't need to mature.

- ✦ 2 sticks plus 2 tablespoons (9 ounces total) butter at room temperature
- ✦ 1½ cups dark brown sugar
- ✦ 4 eggs
- ✦ 3 cups all-purpose flour
- ✦ ¼ teaspoon salt
- ✦ 1 teaspoon ground allspice
- ✦ 1 teaspoon cinnamon
- ✦ ½ teaspoon nutmeg
- ✦ 1½ cups each currants, golden raisins, dark raisins
- ✦ 1⅓ cups soft dried figs, chopped
- ✦ 1¼ cups dates, pitted and chopped
- ✦ 1 cup chopped stoned dried prunes
- ✦ 1¾ cups chopped dried apricots
- ✦ ¾ cup blanched almonds, chopped
- ✦ ⅔ cup plus 4 tablespoons brandy
- ✦ 2 teaspoons instant espresso, mixed with 1 tablespoon water

1 Preheat the oven to 300°F. Grease a round 9- or 10-inch cake pan, and line bottom and sides with several layers of wax paper.

2 In a large bowl, with an electric mixer on *High*, beat the butter and sugar until thick and creamy. Add the eggs, one at a time, beating well after each addition. Sift together the flour, salt, and spices; then fold into the creamed mixture. Add the fruit, almonds, the cup brandy, and espresso, folding in well.

3 Spoon the mixture into the prepared pan, leveling the surface. Place the pan in the center of the oven and bake for 30 minutes. Reduce the temperature to 275°F. and bake for 3½ hours longer or until a tester inserted in the center of the cake comes out clean.

4 Remove the pan from the oven, cover with first a kitchen towel and then a thick bath towel so that the cake will cool slowly.

5 When the cake is cool, prick the top with a skewer and drizzle with the extra brandy. Wrap in wax paper and store in an airtight container. Keep in a cool place for up to 3 months. Makes 30 servings.

TOTAL TIME: 4¾ HOURS PLUS COOLING

Macadamia Biscotti

These popular Italian cookies are twice baked, which gives them a crisp, hard texture and makes them perfect for dipping. Biscotti freeze well, so make an extra batch to have on hand at Christmas.

+ 6 tablespoons unsalted butter, cut up, at room temperature
+ ¾ cup granulated sugar
+ 2 eggs
+ 1 teaspoon vanilla extract
+ 2 teaspoons grated lemon zest
+ 2¼ cups all-purpose flour
+ 1½ teaspoons baking powder
+ ½ teaspoon salt
+ 1 cup macadamia nuts, coarsely chopped

1 Preheat the oven to 350°F. Grease and flour a baking sheet.

2 In a large bowl, with an electric mixer on *High*, beat the butter and sugar until pale and creamy. Beat in the eggs, vanilla, and lemon zest. Add the flour, baking powder, and salt. Blend to combine. Stir in the nuts.

3 Halve the dough and, with lightly oiled hands, roll each half into a log about 2 inches thick and 12 inches long. Place the logs on the baking sheet and bake in the center of the oven for 25 minutes, or until golden.

4 Remove the baking sheet from the oven and place on a rack to cool.

5 Transfer the logs to a breadboard. Using a serrated knife, slice them about ¾ inch thick at a 45° angle. To avoid crumbling, use firm, decisive strokes. Place the slices flat on a baking sheet and return to a 350°F. oven for about 10 minutes, turning once, to dry them.

6 Cool on a rack. The cookies will keep in an airtight container for 2 to 3 weeks. Makes 24 to 30.
TOTAL TIME 1 1/2 HOURS

Almond Tuiles

The curved roof tiles, called tuiles, on the farmhouses of southern France are the inspiration behind these curved almond cookies.

+ 6 tablespoons (3 ounces) unsalted butter
+ ⅓ cup plus 1 tablespoon sugar
+ ½ cup all-purpose flour
+ pinch of salt
+ ⅔ cup slivered or flaked blanched almonds

1 Preheat the oven to 400°F. and grease two baking sheets.

2 In a large bowl, with an electric mixer on *High*, beat the butter and sugar until light and creamy. Beat in the flour with the salt, and stir in the almonds.

3 Drop teaspoonfuls of the dough onto one of the baking sheets, leaving plenty of room for spreading. Flatten each drop with a wet fingertip before putting the baking sheet in the oven.

4 Bake 5 minutes or until golden. Remove from the oven and leave for a few moments to cool on the baking sheet.

5 While the cookies are still warm and pliable, carefully lift each one with a spatula and drape it over a rolling pin to give it the characteristic curved shape. Leave for a minute to harden, then carefully remove and finish cooling on racks. (To make yourself more comfortable with this process, start with just three cookies in the first batch; you will soon get the rhythm of removing and handling the hot tuiles in time to shape them.) Store the cooled cookies in airtight containers. Makes about 24.
TOTAL TIME 40 MINUTES.

Sesame Parmesan Crackers

Served warm, these easy-to-make crackers and sticks are good as a savory snack all by themselves. You can also serve them with spicy salsa.

+ 1 cup all-purpose flour
+ 2½ tablespoons sesame seeds
+ ½ tablespoon salt
+ ¼ cup plus 2 tablespoons grated Parmesan cheese
+ ¾ teaspoon baking soda
+ 3 tablespoons butter, cut up
+ ¼ to ⅓ cup chilled water
+ poppy seeds (optional)

1 Preheat the oven to 350°F.

2 In a medium bowl, combine the flour, sesame seeds, salt, ¼ cup Parmesan cheese, and baking soda. Using your fingers, add the butter, working it in until the mixture resembles fine crumbs. Add enough chilled water to form a stiff dough that you can make into a ball.

3 On a lightly floured surface, roll out the dough to ⅛ inch thick. Using cookie cutters, cut out the cracker shapes. Cut out sesame sticks with a knife and a ruler as a guide. Place on the baking sheet, brush with water, and sprinkle with the 2 tablespoons of Parmesan cheese and the poppy seeds, if you like. Bake for 15 minutes, or until golden and crisp. The crackers and sticks can be stored in an airtight con-tainer for 1 week. Makes about 24 to 36 crackers.

TOTAL TIME 30 TO 40 MINUTES.

Chocolate-Almond Bites

This nutty, chocolate variation on traditional shortbread makes a tasty holiday treat.

- ✦ 2 cups all-purpose flour
- ✦ ½ cup unsweetened cocoa
- ✦ 2 sticks (8 ounces) unsalted butter, at room temperature
- ✦ ½ cup granulated sugar
- ✦ 1 teaspoon vanilla extract
- ✦ ½ teaspoon salt
- ✦ 1 cup toasted almonds, finely chopped
- ✦ sifted confectioners' sugar

1 Preheat the oven to 350°F. Grease a baking sheet.

2 Onto a sheet of wax paper, sift the flour with the cocoa. In a large bowl, with an electric mixer on *High,* beat the butter, sugar, vanilla, and salt until pale and creamy. Beat in the flour mixture, then the almonds.

3 Shape heaped teaspoonfuls of dough into balls and arrange on baking sheet. Bake for 20 to 25 minutes or until firm. Cool briefly on the sheet before removing to a rack.

4 While still slightly warm, dredge the biscuits with confectioners' sugar. Store in an airtight container. They will keep for 5 days. Makes 48 to 60.

TOTAL TIME 45 MINUTES

Snacks and sweets from the oven are shown clockwise from top right: Macadamia Biscotti, Almond Tuiles, Sesame Parmesan Crackers cut in several different shapes, and Chocolate-Almond Bites.

Gingerbread Cottage

Since Victorian days, making a gingerbread house at Christmas time has been a popular project for the whole family to enjoy. This one takes several hours to complete. Youngsters will enjoy the process more if you build it in stages — baking one day, decorating the next, and doing other activities while waiting for the icing to set.

Materials

+ 17 x 14-inch baking sheet
+ Decorating bag with tip with ¼-inch round opening
+ Sharp knife
+ Rolling pin
+ Poster board (cut into pattern pieces shown at right)
+ Two 14 x 10-inch doilies
+ 11 x 11-inch medium-weight cardboard
+ Transparent tape
+ Rubber spatula

Suggested candies:

+ Gumdrops
+ Peppermint rounds
+ Candy-coated chocolate pieces
+ Red cinnamon candies
+ Spearmint leaves
+ Nonpareils
+ Candy buttons

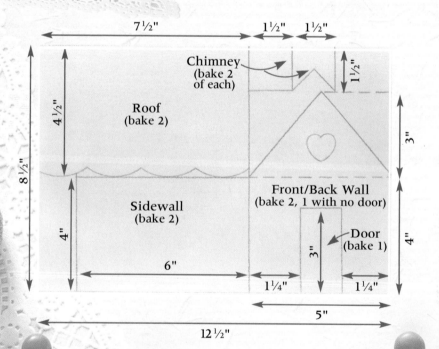

Gingerbread

♦ 1 cup shortening
♦ 1 cup granulated sugar
♦ 1 cup dark molasses
♦ ¼ cup water
♦ 6 cups all-purpose flour
♦ 2 teaspoons each
   ground ginger and
   ground cinnamon
♦ 1 teaspoon salt

For the icing:

♦ 3 large egg whites
♦ ¾ teaspoon cream of tartar
♦ 1 box (16 ounces) confectioners' sugar,
   sifted (4½ cups)
♦ Shredded coconut (optional)

1 In a large bowl, with an electric mixer on *High*, beat the shortening, granulated sugar, molasses, and water until smooth and creamy. In another large bowl, combine the flour, ginger, cinnamon, and salt. Add the dry ingredients to the creamed mixture. Mix to form a stiff dough. Wrap the dough in plastic wrap; refrigerate for 1 hour.

2 Preheat the oven to 350°F. Lightly grease the 17 x 14-inch baking sheet. Place half of the dough on the baking sheet. Using a floured rolling pin, roll out dough to cover baking sheet. (Steady pan by setting it on a dish towel.) Lay pattern pieces on the dough, as shown below, and cut around them with a sharp knife. Carefully remove dough around patterns. Remove poster board. Bake dough pieces for 15 to 20 minutes or until dark brown. Cool on baking sheet for 10 minutes; remove to a rack to finish cooling. Repeat with remaining dough, except omit the door piece and cut back wall without a door.

Assembly

1 To prepare the icing, let the egg whites stand at room temperature for 30 minutes. In a medium-size bowl, with an electric mixer on *High*, beat the egg whites and cream of tartar until frothy. Gradually beat in the confectioners' sugar; continue beating for 7 to 10 minutes or until very stiff. Cover and refrigerate until ready to use.

2 Overlap the 2 doilies on the cardboard; tape in place. Using a rubber spatula, swirl half of the icing almost to the edge of the doilies, building up edges. Sprinkle with coconut (if using); allow to set for 10 minutes. Cover remaining icing with a damp paper towel and refrigerate until needed. Using the decorating bag and tip, pipe icing on the bottom and inside edges of front wall and set in place on base. Pipe icing around the bottom and outside edges of one sidewall and place against the front wall to form an L shape, as shown right. Repeat this procedure with the other side and the

back to form a rectangle. (For added strength, pipe extra icing along the inside joints of cottage.) Allow to set for 1 hour or until icing is very hard.

3 Pipe icing along all top edges, reinforcing corners with extra icing. Position 1 roof piece at a time on the house. With someone holding the roof, reinforce the peak with a line of icing. Allow icing to set for 5 to 10 minutes.

4 To make the chimney, pipe icing on 2 square pieces, as shown below; position the pointed pieces between them to form a square, pressing lightly. When chimney is firm (about 30 minutes), set in place on the roof; reinforce seams and fill in cracks with icing. Set the door in place.

5 Pipe icing decoratively on roof, under eaves, and around window. Decorate with candies as you like,

using icing to glue candies in place. To make icicles, pipe icing strings along the edges of the roof and chimney.

Naturally Good Treats

Years ago, drying was a simple and efficient way to put away food for the winter. Women cut up fruits and vegetables, strung the pieces on thread, hung the strands by the fireplace to dry, and stored them in a cool place.

Introduce the youngsters at your house to the fun of this old-fashioned technique. Start by drying apple slices and toasting pumpkin seeds in your oven. Then, let the kids stir together these two naturally good snacks.

Shake-a-Sack Apple Snack

- ✦ 2 cups Homemade Dried Apples (recipe, below), quartered, or store-bought dried apple chunks
- ✦ 1 package (6 or 7 ounces) dried peaches or apricots, halved and cut into $\frac{1}{2}$-inch pieces
- ✦ 2 cups bite-size wheat-, rice-, corn-, or bran-square cereal
- ✦ 1 cup puffed corn cereal or tiny marshmallows
- ✦ 1 cup coconut
- ✦ 1 cup slivered almonds (optional), toasted

1 In a large heavy-duty plastic bag, combine Homemade Dried Apples, dried peaches, wheat-square cereal, puffed corn cereal, coconut, and almonds (if using). Close bag and seal. Shake until well mixed. Makes 8 to 9 cups.

Homemade Dried Apples

1 Core **4 medium-size tart cooking apples.** Peel apples if you like. Slice the apples into rings, about $\frac{1}{4}$-inch thick.

2 To keep the apple rings from browning, in a large bowl, combine **2 cups cold water** and **2 tablespoons lemon juice.** Add the apple rings, making sure each apple ring gets coated with the water-lemon mixture. Let stand for 5 minutes. Drain well; pat apple rings dry with paper towels.

3 Preheat oven to 300°F. Lightly coat 2 wire racks with **nonstick cooking spray.** Arrange the apple rings in a single layer on the wire racks, making sure rings do not touch or overlap. Set each rack on a baking sheet. Bake for 15 minutes. Reverse positions of the baking sheets in the oven, moving the baking sheet from the top oven rack to the bottom oven rack and vice versa. Bake for 15 minutes more. Turn off the oven. Let the apple rings dry in the oven, with the door closed, for 3 hours. Remove from oven.

4 To store, place apple rings in large heavy-duty plastic bag. Close bag. Makes about 4 cups.

Pumpkin-Patch Party Mix

- ✦ 4 cups air-popped popcorn
- ✦ Toasted Fresh Pumpkin Seeds (recipe, below) or 3 cups shelled unflower nuts
- ✦ 2 cups honey graham cereal, round sweetened bran cereal, or round toasted oat cereal
- ✦ 1½ cups lightly salted dry-roasted mixed nuts or peanuts
- ✦ 1½ cups candy corn or gumdrops
- ✦ 1½ cups raisins

1 In a large bowl, stir together the popped popcorn, Toasted Fresh Pumpkin Seeds, honey graham cereal, mixed nuts, candy corn, and raisins.

2 To store, place in a tightly covered container. Makes about 12 cups.

Toasted Fresh Pumpkin Seeds

1 Remove the seeds from a pumpkin, leaving behind as much of the fiber as you can. Immediately place the seeds in a large bowl of water to avoid any fiber drying on the seeds.

2 Transfer the pumpkin seeds to a colander. Thoroughly rinse the pumpkin seeds under cold running water, rubbing the seeds between your fingers until the pulp and strings are washed off. Drain well.

3 Preheat the oven to 300°F. In a medium-size mixing bowl, combine **3 cups of the pumpkin**

seeds, **2 tablespoons vegetable oil**, and **1 teaspoon salt**; stir to coat well. Spread the seeds onto a baking sheet. Bake for 65 to 70 minutes or until lightly browned and crisp, stirring often to brown the seeds evenly. Cool to room temperature. (The seeds also are good salted and eaten as a snack.) To store, place in a tightly covered container (will keep for 1 week). Makes 3 cups.

Christmas Classics

ENJOY A HEARTWARMING GATHERING OF STORIES AND POEMS,
WITH A SPECIAL PUZZLE AND A PRAYER

The Gift of the Magi

by O. Henry

ONE DOLLAR AND EIGHTY-SEVEN CENTS. That was all. And sixty cents of it was in pennies. Pennies saved one and two at a time by bulldozing the grocer and the vegetable man and the butcher until one's cheeks burned with the silent imputation of parsimony that such close dealing implied. Three times Della counted it. One dollar and eighty-seven cents. And the next day would be Christmas.

There was clearly nothing to do but flop down on the shabby little couch and howl. So Della did it. Which instigates the moral reflection that life is made up of sobs, sniffles, and smiles, with sniffles predominating.

While the mistress of the home is gradually subsiding from the first stage to the second, take a look at the home. A furnished flat at eight dollars per week. It did not exactly beggar description, but it certainly had that word on the lookout for the mendicancy squad.

In the vestibule below was a letter box into which no letter would go, and an electric button from which no mortal finger could coax a ring. Also appertaining thereunto was a card bearing the name "Mr. James Dillingham Young."

The "Dillingham" had been flung to the breeze during a former period of prosperity when its possessor was being paid thirty dollars per week. Now, when the income was shrunk to twenty dollars, the letters of "Dillingham" looked blurred, as though they were thinking seriously of contracting to a modest and unassuming "D." But whenever Mr. James Dillingham Young came home and reached his flat above he was called "Jim" and greatly hugged by Mrs. James Dillingham Young, already introduced to you as Della. Which is all very good.

Della finished her cry and attended to her cheeks with the powder rag. She stood by the window and looked out dully at a gray cat walking a gray fence in a gray backyard. Tomorrow would be Christmas Day and she had only one dollar and eighty-seven cents with which to buy Jim a present. She had been saving every penny she could for months, with this result. Twenty dollars a week doesn't go far. Expenses had been greater than she had calculated. They always are. Only one dollar and eighty-seven cents to buy a present for Jim. Her Jim. Many a happy hour she had spent planning for something nice for him. Something fine and rare and sterling—something just a little bit near to being worthy of the honor of being owned by Jim.

There was a pier glass between the windows of the room. Perhaps you have seen a pier glass in an eight-dollar flat. A very thin and very agile person may, by observing his reflection in a rapid sequence of longitudinal strips, obtain a fairly accurate conception of his looks. Della, being slender, had mastered the art.

Suddenly she whirled from the window and stood before the glass. Her eyes were shining brilliantly, but her face had lost its color within twenty seconds. Rapidly she pulled down her hair and let it fall to its full length.

Now, there were two possessions of the James Dillingham Youngs in which they both took a mighty pride. One was Jim's gold watch that had been his father's and his grandfather's. The other was Della's hair. Had the Queen of Sheba lived in the flat across the air shaft, Della would have let her hair hang out the window someday to dry just to depreciate her Majesty's jewels and gifts. Had King Solomon been the janitor, with all his treasures piled up in the basement, Jim would have pulled out his watch every time he passed, just to see him pluck at his beard from envy.

So now Della's beautiful hair fell about her, rippling and shining like a cascade of brown waters. It reached below her knee and made itself almost a garment for her. And then she did it up again nervously and quickly. Once she faltered for a minute and stood still while a tear or two splashed on the worn red carpet.

On went her old brown jacket; on went her old brown hat. With a whirl of skirts and with the brilliant sparkle still in her eyes, she fluttered out the door and down the stairs to the street.

Where she stopped the sign read: MME. SOFRONIE. HAIR GOODS OF ALL KINDS. One flight up Della ran, and collected herself, panting. Madame, large, too white, chilly, hardly looked the "Sofronie."

"Will you buy my hair?" asked Della.

Only one dollar and eighty-seven cents to buy a present for Jim.

. . . and now she whispered: "Please, God, make him think I am still pretty."

"I buy hair," said Madame. "Take yer hat off and let's have a sight at the looks of it."

Down rippled the brown cascade.

"Twenty dollars," said Madame, lifting the mass with a practiced hand.

"Give it to me quick," said Della.

Oh, and the next two hours tripped by on rosy wings. Forget the hashed metaphor. She was ransacking the stores for Jim's present.

She found it at last. It surely had been made for Jim and no one else. There was no other like it in any of the stores, and she had turned all of them inside out. It was a platinum fob chain, simple and chaste in design, properly proclaiming its value by substance alone and not by meretricious ornamentation—as all good things should do. It was even worthy of The Watch. As soon as she saw it she knew that it must be Jim's. It was like him. Quietness and value—the description applied to both. Twenty-one dollars they took from her for it, and she hurried home with the eighty-seven cents. With that chain on his watch Jim might be properly anxious about the time in any company. Grand as the watch was, he sometimes looked at it on the sly on account of the old leather strap that he used in place of a chain.

When Della reached home her intoxication gave way a little to prudence and reason. She got out her curling irons and lighted the gas and went to work repairing the ravages made by generosity added to love. Which is always a tremendous task, dear friends—a mammoth task.

Within forty minutes her head was covered with tiny close-lying curls that made her look wonderfully like a truant schoolboy. She looked at her reflection in the mirror long, carefully, and critically.

"If Jim doesn't kill me," she said to herself, "before he takes a second look at me, he'll say I look like a Coney Island chorus girl. But what could I do—oh! what could I do with a dollar and eighty-seven cents?"

At seven o'clock the coffee was made and the frying pan was on the back of the stove, hot and ready to cook the chops.

Jim was never late. Della doubled the fob chain in her hand and sat on the corner of the table near the door that he always entered. Then she heard his step on the stair away down on the first flight, and she turned white for just a moment. She had a habit of saying little silent prayers about the simplest everyday things, and now she whispered: "Please, God, make him think I am still pretty."

The door opened and Jim stepped in and closed it. He looked thin and very serious. Poor fellow, he was only twenty-two—and to be burdened with a family! He needed a new overcoat and he was without gloves.

Jim stepped inside the door, as immovable as a setter at the scent of quail. His eyes were fixed upon Della, and there was an expression in them that she could not read, and it terrified her. It was not anger, nor surprise, nor disapproval, nor horror, nor any of the sentiments that she had been prepared for. He simply stared at her fixedly with that peculiar expression on his face.

Della wriggled off the table and went for him.

"Jim, darling," she cried, "don't look at me that way. I had my hair cut off and sold it because I couldn't have lived through Christmas without giving you a present. It'll grow out again—you won't mind, will you? I just had to do it. My hair grows awfully fast. Say 'Merry Christmas!' Jim, and let's be happy. You don't know what a nice—what a beautiful, nice gift I've got for you."

"You've cut off your hair?" asked Jim laboriously, as if he had not arrived at that patent fact yet even after the hardest mental labor.

"Cut it off and sold it," said Della. "Don't you like me just as well anyhow? I'm me without my hair, ain't I?"

Jim looked about the room curiously.

"You say your hair is gone?" he said, with an air almost of idiocy.

"You needn't look for it," said Della. "It's sold, I tell you—sold and gone, too. It's Christmas Eve, boy. Be good to me, for it went for you. Maybe the hairs of my head were numbered," she went on with a sudden serious sweetness, "but nobody could every count my love for you. Shall I put the chops on, Jim?"

Out of his trance Jim seemed quickly to wake. He enfolded his Della. For ten seconds let us regard with discreet scrutiny some inconsequential object in the other direction. Eight dollars a week or a million a year—what is the difference? A mathematician or a wit would give you the wrong answer. The magi brought valuable gifts, but that was not among them. This dark assertion will be illuminated later on.

Jim drew a package from his overcoat pocket and threw it upon the table.

"Don't make any mistake, Dell," he said, "about me. I don't think there's anything in the way of a haircut or a shave or a shampoo that could make me like my girl any less. But if you'll unwrap that package you may see why you had me going awhile at first."

White fingers and nimble tore at the string and paper. And then an

"Say 'Merry Christmas!' Jim, and let's be happy."

ecstatic scream of joy; and then, alas! a quick feminine change to hysterical tears and wails, necessitating the immediate employment of all the comforting powers of the lord of the flat.

For there lay The Combs—the set of combs, side and back, that Della had worshipped for long in a Broadway window. Beautiful combs, pure tortoiseshell, with jeweled rims—just the shade to wear in the beautiful vanished hair. They were expensive combs, she knew, and her heart had simply craved and yearned over them without the least hope of possession. And now they were hers, but the tresses that should have adorned the coveted adornments were gone.

But she hugged them to her bosom, and at length she was able to look up with dim eyes and a smile and say, "My hair grows so fast, Jim!"

And then Della leaped up like a little singed cat and cried, "Oh, oh!"

Jim had not yet seen his beautiful present. She held it out to him eagerly upon her open palm. The dull precious metal seemed to flash with a reflection of her bright and ardent spirit.

"Isn't it a dandy, Jim? I hunted all over town to find it. You'll have to look at the time a hundred times a day now. Give me your watch. I want to see how it looks on it."

Instead of obeying, Jim tumbled down on the couch and put his hands under the back of his head and smiled.

"Dell," said he, "let's put our Christmas presents away and keep 'em awhile. They're too nice to use just at present. I sold the watch to get the money to buy your combs. And now suppose you put the chops on."

The magi, as you know, were wise men—wonderfully wise men—who brought gifts to the Babe in the manger. They invented the art of giving Christmas presents. Being wise, their gifts were no doubt wise ones, possibly bearing the privilege of exchange in case of duplication. And here I have lamely related to you the uneventful chronicle of two foolish children in a flat who most unwisely sacrificed for each other the greatest treasures of their house. But in a last word to the wise of these days let it be said that of all who give gifts these two were the wisest. Of all who give and receive gifts, such as they are wisest. Everywhere they are wisest. They are the magi.

I HEARD A BIRD SING

I heard a bird sing
In the dark of December
A magical thing
And sweet to remember.

"We are nearer to Spring
Than we were in September,"
I heard a bird sing
In the dark of December.

Oliver Herford

'Twas the night before Christmas, when all through
        the house
Not a creature was stirring, not even a mouse;
The stockings were hung by the chimney with care,
In hopes that St. Nicholas soon would be there;
The children were nestled all snug in their beds,
While visions of sugar-plums danced in their heads;
And Mamma in her 'kerchief, and I in my cap,
Had just settled our brains for a long winter's nap;
When out on the lawn there arose such a clatter,
I sprang from the bed to see what what was the matter.
Away to the window I flew like a flash,
Tore open the shutters and threw up the sash.
The moon, on the breast of the new-fallen snow,
Gave the lustre of mid-day to objects below,
When, what to my wondering eyes should appear,
But a miniature sleigh, and eight tiny rein-deer,
With a little old driver, so lively and quick,
I knew in a moment it must be St. Nick.

More rapid than eagles his coursers they came,
And he whistled, and shouted, and called them by name;
"Now, Dasher! now, Dancer! now, Prancer and Vixen!
On, Comet! on, Cupid! on, Donder and Blitzen!
To the top of the porch! to the top of the wall!
Now dash away! dash away! dash away all!"
As dry leaves that before the wild hurricane fly,
When they meet with an obstacle, mount to the sky;
So up to the house-top the coursers they flew,
With the sleigh full of Toys, and St. Nicholas too.
And then, in a twinkling, I heard on the roof
The prancing and pawing of each little hoof —
As I drew in my head, and was turning around,
Down the chimney St. Nicholas came with a bound.
He was dressed all in fur, from his head to his foot,
And his clothes were all tarnished with ashes and soot;
A bundle of Toys he had flung on his back,
And he look'd like a pedlar just opening his pack.
His eyes — how they twinkled! his dimples how merry!
His cheeks were like roses, his nose like a cherry!
His droll little mouth was drawn up like a bow,
And the beard of his chin was as white as the snow;
The stump of a pipe he held tight in his teeth,
And the smoke it encircled his head like a wreath;
He had a broad face and a little round belly,
That shook, when he laughed, like a bowl full of jelly.
He was chubby and plump, a right jolly old elf,
And I laughed, when I saw him, in spite of myself;
A wink of his eye and a twist of his head,
Soon gave me to know I had nothing to dread;

He spoke not a word, but went straight to his work,
And fill'd all the stockings; then turned with a jerk,
And laying his finger aside of his nose,
And giving a nod, up the chimney he rose;
He sprang to his sleigh, to his team gave a whistle,
And away they all flew like the down of a thistle.
But I heard him exclaim, ere he drove out of sight,
"Happy Christmas to all, and to all a good night."

Clement C. Moore,
1862, March 13th originally written
many years ago.

The Legend of the Christmas Rose

by Selma Lagerlöf

Robber Mother, who lived in Robbers' Cave up in Göinge forest, went down to the village one day on a begging tour. Robber Father, who was an outlawed man, did not dare to leave the forest. So his wife took to the road with her five youngsters, each wearing a ragged leathern suit and birch-bark shoes and with a sack on his back as long as himself. Robber Mother and her brood were worse than a pack of wolves, but when she stepped inside the door of a cabin, no one dared refuse to give her whatever she demanded, for she was not above coming back the following night and setting fire to the house if she had not been well received.

As Robber Mother went from house to house and begged, she came one day to Övid, which at that time was a cloister. She rang the bell of the cloister gate and asked for food. The watchman let down a small wicket in the gate and handed her six round bread cakes for herself and each of the five children.

While the mother was standing quietly at the gate, her youngsters were running about. Now one of them came and pulled at her skirt, as a signal that he had discovered something which she ought to come and see, and Robber Mother followed him promptly.

The entire cloister was surrounded by a high and strong wall, but the youngster had managed to find a little back gate which stood ajar. When Robber Mother got there, she pushed the gate open and walked inside without asking leave, as it was her custom to do. Övid Cloister was managed at that time by Abbot Hans, who knew all about herbs. Just within the cloister wall he had planted a little herb garden, and it was into this that the old woman had forced her way.

It was high summertide, and Abbot Hans's garden was so full of flowers that Robber Mother's eyes were fairly dazzled by the blues, reds and yellows. But presently an indulgent smile spread over her features, and she started to walk up a narrow path that lay between many flower beds.

In the garden a lay brother walked about, pulling up weeds. It was he who had left the door in the wall open, that he might throw the weeds on the rubbish heap outside. When he saw Robber Mother coming in, with all five youngsters in tow, he ran toward her and ordered them away. But the beggar woman walked right on as before and took no notice whatever of him.

He thought she had not understood and wanted to take her by the arm and turn her toward the gate. But when she saw his purpose, she straightened herself to her full height. "I am Robber Mother from Göinge forest, so touch me if you dare!" It was obvious that she was certain she would be left in peace.

"I am Robber Mother from Göinge forest, so touch me if you dare!"

And yet the lay brother dared to oppose her. "You must know, Robber Mother, that this is a monks' cloister, and no woman in the land is allowed within these walls."

But Robber Mother walked straight ahead among the little flower beds, looking at the honeysuckles, which were full of deep orange-colored flower clusters. The lay brother knew of no other remedy than to run into the cloister and call for help. He returned with two stalwart monks, and Robber Mother saw that now it meant business! With feet firmly planted on the path she let out a perfect volley of shrieks, and, throwing herself upon the monks, clawed and bit at them, as did the youngsters. The men soon learned that all they could do was to go back into the cloister for reinforcements.

As they ran through the passageway which led to the cloister, they met Abbot Hans, who came rushing out to learn what this noise was about. They told him that Robber Mother from Göinge forest had come into the cloister and confessed they were unable to drive her out without assistance.

Abbot Hans upbraided them for using force and forbade their calling for help. He sent both monks back to their work, and although he was an old

Abbot Hans
had heard it
said that on
every Christmas
Eve the forest
was dressed in
holiday glory.

and fragile man, took with him only the lay brother. When he came out in the garden, Robber Mother was still wandering among the flower beds. He was certain that she had never before seen an herb garden; yet she sauntered leisurely between all the small patches, each with its own species of rare flower, and looked at them as if they were old acquaintances.

Abbot Hans loved his herb garden as much as it was possible for him to love anything earthly and perishable, and he couldn't help liking that the old woman had fought with three monks for the privilege of viewing the garden in peace. He came up to her and asked in a mild tone if the garden pleased her.

Robber Mother turned defiantly toward Abbot Hans, but when she noticed his white hair and bent form, she answered peaceably, "First, when I saw this, I thought I had never seen a prettier garden; but now I see that it can't be compared with one I know of."

When Abbot Hans heard her say that, a faint flush spread over his withered cheek. The lay brother, who was standing close by, immediately began to censure the old woman. "This is Abbot Hans," said he, "who with much care and diligence has gathered the flowers from far and near for his herb garden. We all know that there is not a more beautiful garden to be found, and it is not befitting that you, who live in the wild forest all the year around, should find fault with his work."

"If you could see the garden of which I am thinking you would uproot all the flowers planted here and cast them away like weeds," Robber Mother said.

But the Abbot's assistant was hardly less proud of the flowers than the Abbot himself, and he laughed derisively. "It must be a pretty garden that you have made for yourself amongst the pines in Göinge forest! I'd be willing to wager my soul's salvation that you have never before been within the walls of an herb garden."

Robber Mother grew crimson with rage and she cried out: "It may be true that until today I had not; but you monks, who are holy men, certainly must know that on every Christmas Eve the great Göinge forest is transformed into a beautiful garden, to commemorate the hour of our Lord's birth. We who live in the forest have seen this happen every year. And in that garden I have seen flowers so lovely that I dared not lift my hand to pluck them."

The lay brother wanted to continue the argument, but Abbot Hans gave him a sign to be silent. Ever since his childhood, Abbot Hans had heard it said that on every Christmas Eve the forest was dressed in holiday glory. He had often longed to see it, but he had never had the good fortune. Eagerly he begged Robber Mother that he might come up to the Robbers' Cave on Christmas Eve. If she would send one of her children to show him the way, he could ride up there alone, and he would never betray them—on the contrary, he would reward them, insofar as it lay in his power.

Robber Mother said no at first, for she was thinking of Robber Father and of the peril which might befall him should she permit Abbot Hans to ride up to their cave. At the same time the desire to prove to the monk that the garden which she knew was more beautiful than his got the better of her, and she gave in.

"But more than one follower you cannot take with you," said she, "and you are not to waylay us or trap us, as sure as you are a holy man."

This Abbot Hans promised, and Robber Mother went her way. Abbot Hans commanded the lay brother not to reveal to a soul that which had been agreed upon. He feared that the monks, should they learn of his purpose, would not allow a man of his years to go up to the Robbers' Cave.

Nor did he himself intend to reveal his project to a human being.

Then it happened that Archbishop Absalon from Lund came to Övid and remained through the night. When Abbot Hans was showing him the herb garden, he got to thinking of Robber Mother's visit, and told the Bishop about Robber Father, who these many years had lived as an outlaw in the forest, and asked him for a letter of ransom that the man might lead an honest life among respectable folk.

But the Archbishop replied that he did not care to let the robber loose among honest folk in the villages. It would be best for all that he remain in the forest.

Then Abbot Hans grew zealous and told the Bishop about Göinge forest, which, every year at Yuletide, clothed itself in summer bloom around the Robbers' Cave. "If these bandits are not so bad that God's glories can be made manifest to them, surely we cannot be too wicked to experience the same blessing."

But the lay brother grew more and more anxious, and implored Abbot Hans to turn back . . .

"This much I will promise you, Abbot Hans," the Archbishop said, smiling, "that any day you send me a blossom from the garden in Göinge forest, I will give you letters of ransom for all the outlaws you may choose to plead for."

Abbot Hans thanked Bishop Absalon for his good promise and said that he would surely send him the flower.

The following Christmas Eve Abbot Hans did not sit at home in Övid Cloister, but was on his way to Göinge forest. One of Robber Mother's wild youngsters ran ahead of him, and close behind him was the lay brother.

Abbot Hans had been longing to make this journey, but it was a different matter for the lay brother accompanying him. Abbot Hans was very dear to him, and he would not willingly have allowed another to attend him and watch over him. But he didn't believe that he should see any Christmas Eve garden. He thought the whole thing a snare which Robber Mother had, with great cunning, laid for Abbot Hans, that he might fall into her husband's clutches.

While Abbot Hans was riding toward the forest, he saw that everywhere they were preparing to celebrate Christmas. In every peasant settlement great hunks of meat and bread were being carried from the larders into the cabins, and from the barns came the men with big sheaves of straw to be strewn over the floors. As he rode by the little country churches, he observed that each parson, with his sexton, was busily engaged in decorating his church.

When Abbot Hans saw all these Christmas preparations, his haste increased, thinking of the festivities that awaited him, which were greater than any others. But the lay brother grew more and more anxious, and implored Abbot Hans to turn back and not to throw himself deliberately into the robber's hands.

Abbot Hans went straight ahead, paying no heed. They left the plain behind and came up into desolate and wild forest regions. The farther they rode, the colder it grew, and after a while they came upon snow-covered ground. It turned out to be a long and hazardous ride through the forest. They climbed steep paths, crawled over swamp and marsh, and pushed through windfall and bramble. Just as daylight was waning, the robber boy guided them across a forest meadow, skirted by tall, naked trees and green firs. Back of the meadow loomed a mountain wall, and in this wall they saw a door of thick boards.

Now Abbot Hans dismounted. The child opened the heavy door for him, and he looked into a mountain grotto, with bare stone walls. Robber Mother was seated before a log fire that burned in the middle of the floor. Alongside the walls were beds of pine and moss, and on one of these beds lay Robber Father asleep.

"Come in, you out there!" shouted Robber Mother without rising. Abbot Hans walked boldly into the cave, and the lay brother followed. Here were wretchedness and poverty! and nothing was done to celebrate Christmas. Robber Mother had neither brewed nor baked; neither had she washed nor scoured. The youngsters were lying on the floor around a kettle, eating; but no better food was provided for them than a watery gruel.

Robber Mother spoke in a tone as haughty and dictatorial as any well-to-do peasant woman. "Sit down by the fire and warm yourself, Abbot Hans," said she; "and if you have food with you, eat, for the food we in the forest prepare you wouldn't care to taste. And if you are tired after the long journey, you can lie down on one of these beds to sleep. I shall awaken you in time to see that which you have come up here to see."

Abbot Hans obeyed Robber Mother and brought forth his food sack; but he was so fatigued after the journey he was hardly able to eat, and as soon as he could stretch himself on the bed, he fell asleep.

Gradually fatigue got the better of the lay brother, too, and he dropped into a doze. When he woke up, he saw that Abbot Hans had left his bed and was sitting by the fire talking with Robber Mother. The outlawed robber sat also by the fire, pretending not to be listening. He was a tall, rawboned man with a dull, sluggish appearance.

Abbot Hans was telling Robber Mother all about the Christmas preparations he had seen on the journey, reminding her of Christmas feasts and games which she must have known in her youth, when she lived at peace with mankind. "I'm sorry for your children, who can never run on the village street in holiday dress or tumble in the Christmas straw," said he.

At first Robber Mother answered in short, gruff sentences, but by degrees she listened more intently. Suddenly Robber Father turned toward Abbot Hans and shook his fist. "You miserable monk! did you come here to coax from me my wife and children? Don't you know that I am an outlaw and may not leave the forest?"

Abbot Hans looked him fearlessly in the eyes. "It is my purpose to get a letter of ransom for you from Archbishop Absalon," said he. He had hardly finished speaking when the robber and his wife burst out laughing. They

"I'm sorry for your children, who can never run on the village street in holiday dress or tumble in the Christmas straw."

Abbot Hans

saw that the snow

had vanished

from the ground

and the earth

began to take on a

green covering.

knew well enough the kind of mercy a forest robber could expect from Bishop Absalon!

"If I get a letter of ransom from Absalon," said Robber Father, "then I'll promise you that never again will I steal so much as a goose."

Suddenly Robber Mother rose. "We are forgetting to look at the forest," she said. "Now I can hear, even in this cave, how the Christmas bells are ringing."

The words were barely uttered when they all sprang up and rushed out. But in the forest it was still dark night and bleak winter. The only thing they marked was a distant clang borne on a light south wind. "How can this bell ringing ever awaken the dead forest?" thought Abbot Hans. For now, as he stood out in the winter darkness, he thought it impossible that a summer garden could spring up here.

When the bells had been ringing a few moments, a sudden illumination penetrated the forest; it pushed its way forward between the stark trees, like a shimmering mist. Then Abbot Hans saw that the snow had vanished from the ground and the earth began to take on a green covering. The ferns shot up their fronds, rolled like a bishop's staff. The heather that grew on the stony hills quickly dressed itself in new bloom, the moss-tufts thickened and raised themselves, and the spring blossoms shot upward their swelling buds.

Abbot Hans's heart beat fast as he marked the first signs of the forest's awakening. "Old man that I am, shall I behold such a miracle?" thought he, and the tears wanted to spring to his eyes. Then it grew so hazy that he feared the darkness would once more cover the earth; but almost immediately there came a new wave of light. The leaves of the trees burst into bloom, crossbeaks hopped from branch to branch, the woodpeckers hammered on the limbs, and a flock of paradise starlings lighted in fir tops to rest, the brilliant red tips of their feathers glittering like so many jewels.

Again, all was dark for an instant, but soon there came a new light wave. A fresh, warm south wind blew and scattered over the forest meadow little seeds that took root and sprang up the instant they touched the earth. Cranes and wild geese shrieked in the air, and the baby squirrels began playing on the branches of the trees. The juniper berries changed color every second, and forest flowers covered the ground till it was all red, blue and yellow.

Abbot Hans bent down to the earth and broke off a wild strawberry blossom, and, as he straightened up, the berry ripened in his hand.

The mother fox came out of her lair with a litter of black-legged young. She went up to Robber Mother and scratched at her skirt, and Robber Mother bent down to her and praised her young.

Robber Mother's own youngsters cried out in delight. They stuffed themselves with wild strawberries that hung on the bushes, large as pine cones. One of them played with a litter of young hares; another ran a race with some young crows, which had hopped from their nest; a third caught up an adder from the ground and wound it around his neck and arm.

Robber Father was standing out on a marsh eating raspberries. When he glanced up, a big black bear stood beside him. "Keep to your own ground, you!" Robber Father said. "This is my turf." The huge bear turned around and lumbered off in another direction.

New waves of warmth and light kept coming, and now golden pollen fairly flew in the air. The beehive in a hollow oak was already so full of honey that it dripped down on the trunk of the tree. The loveliest roses climbed up the mountain wall, and from the forest meadow sprang flowers as large as human faces.

Abbot Hans thought of the flower he was to pluck for Bishop Absalon; but each new flower that appeared was more beautiful than the others, and he wanted to choose the most beautiful of all.

Wave upon wave kept coming until the air was so filled with light that it glittered.

Wave upon wave kept coming until the air was so filled with light that it glittered. All the life and beauty and joy of summer smiled on Abbot Hans. He felt a celestial atmosphere enfolding him, and tremblingly he began to anticipate, now that earth's joys had come, the glories of heaven approaching, glories such that the heart wanted to stop beating and the soul longed to soar away into the Eternal. From far in the distance faint harp tones were heard, and celestial song, like a soft murmur, reached him. Abbot Hans clasped his hands and dropped to his knees, his face radiant with bliss.

But in the mind of the lay brother who had accompanied Abbot Hans there were dark thoughts. "This cannot be a true miracle," he thought, "since it is revealed to malefactors. This does not come from God, but has its origin in witchcraft and is sent hither by Satan."

Now Abbot Hans saw the bright forms of the angel throng through the forest branches. The lay brother saw them, too; but back of all this wondrous beauty he saw only some dread evil.

All the while the birds had been circling around the head of Abbot Hans, and they let him take them in his hands. But they were afraid of the lay brother. Yet when a little forest dove saw that the angels were nearing, she plucked up courage and flew down on the lay brother's shoulder and laid her head against his cheek.

Just then the angels were so near that Abbot Hans felt the feathery touch of their great wings . . .

Then it appeared to him as if sorcery were come right upon him, to tempt and corrupt him. He struck with his hand at the forest dove and cried in such a loud voice that it rang throughout the forest, "Go thou back to hell, whence thou art come!"

Just then the angels were so near that Abbot Hans felt the feathery touch of their great wings, and he bowed down to earth in reverent greeting.

But when the lay brother's words sounded, their song was hushed and the holy guests turned in flight. At the same time the light and the mild warmth vanished. Darkness sank over the earth, like a coverlet; frost came, all the growths shriveled up; the animals and birds hastened away; the rushing of streams was hushed; the leaves dropped from the trees, rustling like rain.

Abbot Hans felt how his heart, which had but lately swelled with bliss, was now contracting with insufferable agony. "I can never outlive this," thought he, "that the angels from heaven had been so close to me, that they wanted to sing Christmas carols for me and were driven to flight."

Then he remembered the flower he had promised Bishop Absalon, and at the last moment he fumbled among the leaves and moss to try and find a blossom. But he sensed how the ground under his fingers froze and how the white snow came gliding over it. Then his heart caused him ever greater anguish. He could not rise, but fell prostrate on the ground and lay there.

When the robber folk and the lay brother had groped their way back to the cave, they missed Abbot Hans. They took torches with them and went out to search for him. They found him dead upon the coverlet of snow. Then the lay brother began weeping, for he understood that it was he who had killed Abbot Hans because he had dashed from him the cup of happiness.

When Abbot Hans had been carried down to Övid, those who took charge of the dead saw that he held his right hand locked tight around something which he must have grasped at the moment of death. It was a pair of white root bulbs, which he had torn from among the moss and leaves.

When the lay brother saw the bulbs, he took them and planted them in Abbot Hans's herb garden. He guarded them the whole year to see if any flower would spring from them. But in vain he waited through the spring, the summer and the autumn. Finally, when winter had set in and all the leaves and the flowers were dead, he ceased caring for them.

But when Christmas Eve came again, he was so strongly reminded of Abbot Hans that he wandered out into the garden to think of him. And look! as he came to the spot where he had planted the bare root bulbs, he saw that from them had sprung flourishing green stalks, which bore beautiful flowers with silver white leaves.

He called out all the monks, and when they saw that this plant bloomed on Christmas Eve, when all the other growths were as if dead, they understood that this flower had in truth been plucked by Abbot Hans from the Christmas garden in Göinge forest. Then the lay brother asked the monks if he might take a few blossoms to Bishop Absalon. When he appeared before the Archbishop, he gave him the flowers and said: "Abbot Hans sends you these. They are the flowers he promised to pick for you from the garden in Göinge forest."

When Bishop Absalon beheld the flowers, which had sprung from the earth in darkest winter, and heard the words, he turned pale as if he had met a ghost. He sat in silence a moment; thereupon he said, "Abbot Hans has faithfully kept his word and I shall also keep mine." And he ordered that a letter of ransom be drawn up for the outlawed robber.

He handed the letter to the lay brother, who departed at once for the Robbers' Cave. When he stepped in there on Christmas Day, the robber came toward him with axe uplifted. "I'd like to hack you monks into bits, as many as you are!" said he. "It must be your fault that Göinge forest did not last night dress itself in Christmas bloom."

"Hereafter you and your children shall celebrate your Christmas among people, just as Abbot Hans wished to have it."

"The fault is mine alone," said the lay brother, "and I will gladly die for it. But first I must deliver a message from Abbot Hans." And he drew forth the Bishop's letter and told the man that he was free. "Hereafter you and your children shall celebrate your Christmas among people, just as Abbot Hans wished to have it," said he.

The Robber Father stood there pale and speechless, but Robber Mother said in his name, "Abbot Hans has indeed kept his word, and Robber Father will keep his."

When the robber and his wife left the cave, the lay brother moved in and lived alone in the forest, in constant meditation and prayer that his hardheartedness might be forgiven him.

But Göinge forest never again celebrated the hour of our Saviour's birth; and all its glory, there lives today only the plant which Abbot Hans had plucked. It has been named *Christmas Rose*. And each year at Christmastide she sends forth from the earth her green stalks and white blossoms, as if she never could forget that she had once grown in the great Christmas garden at Göinge forest.

Heaven Cannot Hold Him

In the bleak midwinter
  Frosty wind made moan,
Earth stood hard as iron,
  Water like a stone;
Snow had fallen, snow on snow,
  Snow on snow,
In the bleak midwinter
  Long ago.

Our God, Heaven cannot hold Him
  Nor earth sustain;
Heaven and earth shall flee away
  When He comes to reign:
In the bleak midwinter
  A stable-place sufficed
The Lord God Almighty
  Jesus Christ.

Enough for Him, whom cherubim
  Worship night and day,
A breastful of milk
  And a mangerful of hay;
Enough for Him, whom angels
  Fall down before,
The ox and ass and camel
  Which adore.

Angels and archangels
  May have gathered there,
Cherubim and seraphim
  Thronged the air;
But only His mother
  In her maiden bliss
Worshipped the Beloved
  With a kiss.

What can I give Him,
  Poor as I am?
If I were a shepherd
  I would bring a lamb
If I were a Wise Man
  I would do my part,—
Yet what I can I give Him,
  Give my heart.

Christina Rossetti (1830-1894)

The Fir Tree

by Hans Christian Andersen

OUT IN THE FOREST stood a pretty little Fir Tree. It had a good place; it could have sunlight, air there was in plenty, and all around grew many larger comrades—pines as well as firs. But the little Fir Tree wished ardently to become greater. It did not care for the warm sun and the fresh air; it took no notice of the peasant children, who went about talking together, when they had come out to look for strawberries and raspberries. Often they came with a whole potful, or had strung berries on a straw; then they would sit down by the little Fir Tree and say, "How pretty and small that one is!" and the Fir Tree did not like to hear that at all.

Next year he had grown a great joint, and the following year he was longer still, for in fir trees one can always tell by the number of rings they have how many years they have been growing.

"Oh, if I were only as great a tree as the others!" sighed the little Fir. "Then I would spread my branches far around and look out from my crown into the wide world. The birds would then build nests in my boughs, and when the wind blew I could nod just as grandly as the others yonder."

He took no pleasure in the sunshine, in the birds, and in the red clouds that went sailing over him morning and evening.

When it was winter, the snow lay all around, white and sparkling, a hare would often come jumping along, and spring right over the little Fir Tree. Oh! This made him so angry. But two winters went by, and when the third came the little Tree had grown so tall that the hare was obliged to run around it.

Oh! To grow, to grow, and become old; that's the only fine thing in the world, thought the Tree.

In the autumn woodcutters always came and felled a few of the largest trees; that was done this year, too, and the little Fir Tree, that was now quite well grown, shuddered with fear, for the great stately trees fell to the ground with a crash, and their branches were cut off, so that the trees looked quite naked, long, and slender—they could hardly be recognized. But then they were laid upon wagons, and horses dragged them away out of the wood. Where were they going? What destiny awaited them?

In the spring when the Swallows and the Stork came, the Tree asked them, "Do you know where they were taken? Did you not meet them?"

The Swallows knew nothing about it, but the Stork looked thoughtful, nodded his head, and said, "Yes, I think so. I met many new ships when I flew out of Egypt; on the ships were stately masts; I fancy these were the trees. They smelled like fir. I can assure you they're stately—very stately."

"Oh, that I were only big enough to go over the sea! What kind of thing is this sea, and how does it look?"

"It would take too long to explain all that," said the Stork, and he went away.

"Rejoice in thy youth," said the Sunbeams; "rejoice in thy fresh growth, and in the young life that is within thee."

And the Wind kissed the Tree, and the Dew wept tears upon it; but the Fir Tree did not understand about that.

When Christmastime approached, quite young trees were felled, sometimes trees which were neither so old nor so large as this Fir Tree, that never rested, but always wanted to go away. These young trees, which were always the most beautiful, kept all their branches; they were put upon wagons, and horses dragged them away out of the wood.

"Where are they all going?" asked the Fir Tree. "They are not greater than I—indeed, one of them was much smaller. Why do they keep all their branches? Whither are they taken?"

"We know that! We know that!" chirped the Sparrows. "Yonder in the town we looked in at the windows. We know where they go. Oh! They are dressed up in the greatest pomp and splendor that can be imagined. We have looked in at the windows, and have perceived that they are planted in the middle of a warm room, and adorned with the most beautiful things— gilt apples, honey cakes, playthings, and many hundreds of candles."

"And then?" asked the Fir Tree, and trembled through all its branches. "And then? What happens then?"

"Why, we have not seen anything more. But it is incomparable."

"Perhaps I may be destined to tread this glorious path one day!" cried the Fir Tree rejoicingly. "That is even better than traveling across the sea. How painfully I long for it! If it were only Christmas now! Now I am great and grown up, like the rest who were led away last year. Oh, if I were only on the carriage! If I were only in the warm room, among all the pomp and splendor! And then? Yes, then something even better will come, something far more charming, or else why should they adorn me so? There must be something grander, something greater still to come; but what? Oh! I'm suffering. I'm longing! I don't know myself what is the matter with me!"

"If I were only in the warm room, among all the pomp and splendor!"

"Rejoice in us," said the Air and Sunshine. "Rejoice in thy fresh youth here in the woodland."

But the Fir Tree did not rejoice at all, but it grew and grew; winter and summer it stood there, green, dark green. The people who saw it said, "That's a handsome tree!" and at Christmastime it was felled before any of the others. The axe cut deep into its marrow, and the Tree fell to the ground with a sigh; it felt a pain, a sensation of faintness, and could not think at all of happiness, for it was sad at parting from its home, from the place where it had grown up; it knew that it should never again see the dear old companions, the little bushes and flowers all around—perhaps not even the birds. The parting was not at all agreeable.

The Tree only came to itself when it was unloaded in a yard, with other trees, and heard a man say, "This one is famous; we want only this one!"

Now two servants came in gay liveries and carried the Fir Tree into a large, beautiful salon. All around the walls hung pictures, and by the great stove stood large Chinese vases with lions on the covers; there were rocking chairs, silken sofas, great tables covered with picture books, and toys worth a

. . . and more than a hundred little candles, red, white, and blue, were fastened to the different boughs.

hundred times a hundred dollars, at least the children said so. And the Fir Tree was put into a great tub filled with sand; but no one could see that it was a tub, for it was hung round with green cloth, and stood on a large, many-colored carpet. Oh, how the Tree trembled! What was to happen now? The servants, and the young ladies also, decked it out. On one branch they hung little nets, cut out of colored paper; every net was filled with sweetmeats; golden apples and walnuts hung down, as if they grew there, and more than a hundred little candles, red, white, and blue, were fastened to the different boughs. Dolls that looked exactly like real people—the Tree had never seen such before—swung among the foliage, and high on the summit of the Tree was fixed a tinsel star. It was splendid, particularly splendid.

"This evening," said all, "this evening it will shine."

Oh, thought the Tree, that it were evening already! Oh, that the lights may soon be lit up! When may that be done? Will the Sparrows fly against the panes? Shall I grow fast here, and stand adorned in summer and winter?

Yes, he did not guess badly. But he had a complete backache from mere longing, and backache is just as bad for a tree as a headache for a person.

At last the candles were lighted. What a brilliance, what a splendor! The Tree trembled so in all its branches that one of the candles set fire to a green twig, and it was scorched.

"Heaven preserve us!" cried the young ladies; and they hastily put the fire out.

Now the Tree might not even tremble. Oh, that was terrible! It was so afraid of setting fire to some of its ornaments, and it was quite bewildered with all the brilliance. And now the folding doors were thrown wide open, and a number of children rushed in as if they would have overturned the whole Tree; the older people followed more deliberately. The little ones stood quite silent, but only for a minute; then they shouted till the room rang; they danced gleefully round the Tree, and one present after another was plucked from it.

What are they about? thought the Tree. What's going to be done?

And the candles burned down to the twigs, and as they burned down they were extinguished, and then the children received permission to plunder the Tree. Oh! They rushed upon it, so that every branch cracked again: if it had not been fastened by the top and by the golden star to the ceiling, it would have fallen down.

The children danced about with their pretty toys. No one looked at the Tree except one old man, who came up and peeped among the branches, but only to see if a fig or an apple had not been forgotten.

"A story! A story!" shouted the children; and they drew a little fat man toward the Tree; and he sat down just beneath it—"for then we shall be in the greenwood," said he, "and the Tree may have the advantage of listening to my tale. But I can only tell one. Will you hear the story of Ivede-Avede, or of Klumpey-Dumpey, who fell downstairs, and still was raised up to honor and married the princess?"

"Ivede-Avede!" cried some. "Klumpey-Dumpey!" cried others, and there was a great crying and shouting. Only the Fir Tree was quite silent, and

thought, Shall I not be in it? Shall I have nothing to do in it? But he had been in the evening's amusement, and had done what was required of him.

And the fat man told about Klumpey-Dumpey, who fell downstairs and yet was raised to honor and married a princess. And the children clapped their hands and cried, "Tell another! Tell another!" and they wanted to hear about Ivede-Avede; but they only got the story of Klumpey-Dumpey. The Fir Tree stood quite silent and thoughtful; never had the birds in the wood told such a story as that. Klumpey-Dumpey fell downstairs, and yet came to honor and married a princess!

Yes, so it happens in the world! thought the Fir Tree, and believed it must be true, because that was such a nice man who told it.

Well, who can know? Perhaps I shall fall downstairs, too, and marry a princess! And it looked forward with pleasure to being adorned again, the next evening, with candles and toys, gold and fruit. Tomorrow I shall not tremble, it thought. I shall rejoice in all my splendor. Tomorrow I shall hear the story of Klumpey-Dumpey again, and perhaps that of Ivede-Avede, too.

And the Tree stood all night, quiet and thoughtful.

"A story! A story!" shouted the children; and they drew a little fat man toward the Tree . . .

Now the Tree

stood quite

hidden away, and

the supposition

is that

it was quite

forgotten.

In the morning the servants and the chambermaid came in.

Now my splendor will begin afresh, thought the Tree. But they dragged him out of the room and upstairs to the garret, and here they put him in a dark corner where no daylight shone. What's the meaning of this? thought the Tree. What am I to do here? What is to happen?

And he leaned against the wall, and thought, and thought. And he had time enough, for days and nights went by, and nobody came up; and when at length someone came, it was only to put some great boxes in a corner. Now the Tree stood quite hidden away, and the supposition is that it was quite forgotten.

Now it's winter outside, thought the Tree. The earth is hard and covered with snow, and people cannot plant me; therefore I suppose I'm to be sheltered here until spring comes. How considerate that is! How good people are! If it were only not so dark here, and so terribly solitary! Not even a little hare? That was pretty out there in the wood, when the snow lay thick and the hare sprang past; yes, even when he jumped over me; but then I did not like it. It is terribly lonely up here!

"Piep! Piep!" said a little Mouse, and crept forward, and then came another little one. They smelled at the Fir Tree and then slipped among the branches.

"It's horribly cold," said the two little Mice, "or else it would be comfortable here. Don't you think so, old Fir Tree?"

"I'm not old at all," said the Fir Tree. "There are many much older than I."

"Where do you come from?" asked the Mice. "And what do you know?" They were dreadfully inquisitive. "Tell us about the most beautiful spot on earth. Have you been there? Have you been in the storeroom, where cheeses lie on the shelves, and hams hang from the ceiling, where one dances on tallow candles, and goes in thin and comes out fat?"

"I don't know that," replied the Tree; "but I know the wood, where the sun shines and the birds sing."

And then it told all about its youth.

And the little Mice had never heard anything of the kind; and they listened and said, "What a number of things you have seen! How happy you must have been!"

"I?" replied the Fir Tree; and it thought about what it had told. "Yes, those were really quite happy times." But then he told of the Christmas Eve, when he had been hung with sweatmeats and candles.

"Oh!" said the little Mice. "How happy you have been, you old Fir Tree."

"I'm not old at all," said the Tree. "I only came out of the wood this winter. I'm only rather backward in my growth."

"What splendid stories you can tell!" said the little Mice.

And the next night they came with four other little Mice, to hear what the Tree had to relate; and the more it said, the more clearly did it remember everything, and thought, Those were quite merry days! But they may come again. Klumpey-Dumpey fell downstairs, and yet he married a princess. Perhaps I shall marry a princess, too! And the Fir Tree thought of a pretty little Birch Tree that grew out in the forest; for the Fir Tree, that Birch was a real princess.

"Who's Klumpey-Dumpey?" asked the little Mice.

And then the Fir Tree told the whole story. It could remember every single word; and the little Mice were ready to leap to the very top of the Tree with pleasure. Next night a great many more Mice came, and on Sunday two Rats even appeared; but these thought the story was not pretty, and the little Mice were sorry for that, for now they also did not like it so much as before.

"Do you know only one story?" asked the Rats.

"Only that one," replied the Tree. "I heard that on the happiest evening of my life; I did not think then how happy I was."

"That's a very miserable story. Don't you know any about bacon and tallow candles—a storeroom story?"

"No," said the Tree.

Everything passed so quickly that the Tree quite forgot to look at itself, there was so much to look at all round.

"Then we'd rather not hear you," said the Rats. And they went back to their own people.

The little Mice at last stayed away also; and then the Tree sighed and said, "It was very nice when they sat round me, the merry little Mice, and listened when I spoke to them. Now that's past, too. But I shall remember to be pleased when they take me out."

But when did that happen? Why, it was one morning that people came and rummaged in the garret; the boxes were put away, and the Tree brought out; they certainly threw him rather roughly on the floor, but a servant dragged him away at once to the stairs, where the daylight shone.

Now life is beginning again! thought the Tree.

It felt the fresh air and the first sunbeam, and now it was out in the courtyard. Everything passed so quickly that the Tree quite forgot to look at itself, there was so much to look at all round. The courtyard was close to a garden, and here everything was blooming; the roses hung fresh over the paling, the linden trees were in blossom, and the Swallows cried, "Quinze-wit! Quinze-wit! My husband's come!" But it was not the Fir Tree that they meant.

"Now I shall live!" said the Tree rejoicingly, and spread its branches far out; but, alas! they were all withered and yellow; and it lay in the corner among nettles and weeds. The tinsel star, still upon it, shone in the bright sunshine.

In the courtyard a couple of the merry children were playing who had danced round the tree at Christmastime and had rejoiced over it. One of the youngest ran up and tore off the golden star.

"Look what is sticking to the ugly old Fir Tree!" said the child, and he trod upon the branches till they cracked again under his boots.

And the Tree looked at all the blooming flowers and the splendor of the garden, and then looked at itself, and wished it had remained in the dark corner of the garret; it thought of its fresh youth in the wood, of the merry Christmas Eve, and of the little Mice which had listened so pleasantly to the story of Klumpey-Dumpey.

"Past! Past!" said the old Tree. "Had I but rejoiced when I could have done so! Past! Past!"

And the servant came and chopped the Tree into little pieces; a whole bundle lay there; it blazed brightly under the great brewing copper, and it sighed deeply, and each sigh was like a little shot; and the children who were at play there ran up and seated themselves at the fire, looked into it, and cried, "Puff! Puff!" But at each explosion, which was a deep sigh, the Tree thought of a summer day in the woods, or of a winter night there, when the stars beamed; he thought of Christmas Eve and of Klumpey-Dumpey, the only story he had ever heard or known how to tell; and then the Tree was burned.

. . . the Tree thought of a summer day in the woods, or of a winter night there, when the stars beamed . . .

The boys played in the garden, and the youngest had on his breast a golden star, which the Tree had worn on its happiest evening. Now that was past, and the Tree's life was past, and the story is past, too: past! past! And that's the way with all stories.

A Letter from Santa Claus

by Mark Twain

Palace of St. Nicholas
In the Moon
Christmas Morning

MY DEAR SUSIE CLEMENS:

I have received and read all the letters which you and your little sister have written me by the hand of your mother and your nurses; I have also read those which you little people have written me with your own hands—for although you did not use any characters that are in grown peoples' alphabet, you used the characters that all children in all lands on earth and in the twinkling stars use; and as all my subjects in the moon are children and use no character but that, you will easily understand that I can read your and your baby sister's jagged and fantastic marks without any trouble at all. But I had trouble with those letters which you dictated through your mother and the nurses, for I am a foreigner and cannot read English writing well. You will find that I made no mistakes about the things which you and the baby ordered in your own letters—I went down your chimney at midnight when you were asleep and delivered them all myself—and kissed both of you, too, because you are good children, well trained, nice mannered, and about the most obedient little people I ever saw. But in the letter which you dictated there were some words which I could not make out for certain, and one or two small orders which I could not fill because we ran out of stock. Our last lot of kitchen furniture for dolls has just gone to a very poor little child in the North Star away up in the cold country above the Big Dipper. Your mama can show you that star and you will say: "Little Snow Flake," (for that is the child's name) "I'm glad you got that furniture, for you need it more than I." That is, you must *write* that, with your own hand, and Snow Flake will write you an answer. If you only spoke it she wouldn't hear you. Make your letter light and thin, for the distance is great and the postage very heavy.

There was a word or two in your mama's letter which I couldn't be certain of. I took it to be "a trunk full of doll's clothes." Is that it? I will call at your kitchen door about nine o'clock this morning to inquire. But I must not see anybody and I must not speak to anybody but you. When the kitchen

Clara, Samuel and Susie Clemens, 1877

If my boot

should leave a

stain on the

marble . . . Leave

it there always

in memory of

my visit . . .

doorbell rings, George must be blindfolded and sent to open the door. Then he must go back to the dining room or the china closet and take the cook with him. You must tell George he must walk on tiptoe and not speak—otherwise he will die someday. Then you must go up to the nursery and stand on a chair or the nurse's bed and put your ear to the speaking tube that leads down to the kitchen and when I whistle through it you must speak in the tube and say, "Welcome, Santa Claus!" Then I will ask whether it was a trunk you ordered or not. If you say it was, I shall ask you what *color* you want the trunk to be. Your mama will help you to name a nice color and then you must tell me every single thing in detail which you want the trunk to contain. Then when I say "Good-by and a merry Christmas to my little Susie Clemens," you must say "Good-by, good old Santa Claus, I thank you very much and please tell that little Snow Flake I will look at her star tonight and she must look down here—I will be right in the west bay window; and every fine night I will look at her star and say, 'I know somebody up there and *like* her, too.'" Then you must go down into the library and make George close all the doors that open into the main hall, and everybody must keep still for a little while. I will go to the moon and get those things and in a few minutes I will come down the chimney that belongs to the fireplace that is in the hall—if it is a trunk you want—because I couldn't get such a thing as a trunk down the nursery chimney, you know.

People may talk if they want, until they hear my footsteps in the hall. Then you tell them to keep quiet a little while till I go back up the chimney. Maybe you will not hear my footsteps at all—so you may go now and then and peep through the dining-room doors, and by and by you will see that thing which you want, right under the piano in the drawing room—for I shall put it there. If I should leave any snow in the hall, you must tell George to sweep it into the fireplace, for I haven't time to do such things. George must not use a broom, but a rag—else he will die someday. You must watch George and not let him run into danger. If my boot should leave a stain on the marble, George must not holystone it away. Leave it there always in memory of my visit; and whenever you look at it or show it to anybody you must let it remind you to be a good little girl. Whenever you are naughty and somebody points to that mark which your good old Santa Claus's boot made on the marble, what will you say, little sweetheart?

Good-by for a few minutes, till I come down to the world and ring the kitchen doorbell.

Your loving SANTA CLAUS
Whom people sometimes call "The Man in the Moon"

It Pays to Enrich Your Word Power®

The Christmas season is rich with songs and readings passed down through generations. Each year, their melodies and cadences help renew the spirit of the season. But take a closer look. How many of the words we've heard since childhood do you really know? Try this quiz about words associated with Christmas, then check your answers by turning to the next page. Whatever your score, you are sure to find new meanings to the holidays this year.

1. **cherubim** *(n.)*—A: ornaments. B: reindeer. C: angels. D: rare fruit.

2. **incarnate** *(adj.)*—A: ancient. B: in human form. C: holy. D: whitened.

3. **exultation** *(n.)*—A: uprising. B: release. C: crowning. D: great joy.

4. **Emmanuel** *(n.)*—A: judge. B: Messiah. C: messenger. D: naysayer.

5. **yule** *(n.)*—A: shepherd's staff. B: Christmas. C: peace. D: gift.

6. **wassail** *(n.)*—A: spiced ale. B: cart. C: prayer. D: pudding.

7. **advent** *(n.)*—A: assembly. B: prediction. C: arrival. D: addition.

8. **cloven** *(adj.)*—A: wearing jewels. B: poor. C: spiced. D: split apart.

9. **laud** *(v.)*—A: to cover. B: decorate. C: praise. D: doubt.

10. **nowel** *(n.)*—A: announcement. B: exclamation of joy. C: lullaby. D: star.

11. **frankincense** *(n.)*—A: good advice. B: herb. C: incense. D: nonsense.

12. **natal** *(adj.)*—relating to A: night. B: donkeys. C: water. D: birth.

13. **epiphany** *(n.)*—A: sudden revelation. B: uncertainty. C: ringing of chimes. D: stillness.

14. **deck** *(v.)*—A: to adorn. B: paint. C: clean. D: fill up.

15. **mirth** *(n.)*—A: water pitcher. B: merriment. C: hot cider. D: hopelessness.

16. **mean** *(adj.)*—A: prosperous. B: unselfish. C: new. D: shabby.

17. **Magi** *(n.)*—A: shepherds. B: Wise Men. C: servants. D: Northern lights.

18. **firmament** *(n.)*—A: sky. B: desert. C: globe. D: rainbow.

19. **ransom** *(v.)*—A: to enslave. B: feed. C: free. D: torment.

20. **nigh** *(adj.)*—A: floating. B: close. C: surprising. D: far off.

21. **waits** *(n.)*—A: couriers. B: guards. C: farmers. D: singers.

22. **crèche** *(n.)*—A: cradle. B: halo. C: Nativity scene. D: group of animals.

23. **troll** *(v.)*—A: to walk slowly. B: carry. C: sing lustily. D: light up.

24. **sugarplum** *(n.)*—A: evergreen tree. B: fruit. C: spice. D: candy.

25. **boxing day** *(n.)*—A: children's party. B: day to return presents. C: weekday after Christmas. D: day before Christmas.

26. **tidings** *(n.)*—A: premonition. B: gifts. C: singing. D: news.

27. **reconciled** *(adj.)*—A: remembered. B: brought into harmony. C: hoped for. D: conflicted.

28. **diadem** *(n.)*—A: gemstone. B: shaft of light. C: trumpet. D: crown.

29. **manger** *(n.)*—A: barn. B: blanket. C: trough. D: farm.

30. **courser** *(n.)*—A: swift runner. B: believer. C: shooting star. D: marker.

WORD POWER® ANSWERS

1. **cherubim**—C: Angels, specifically those symbolizing wisdom and light (versus seraphim, representing love), often depicted in art as chubby, rosy-faced children with wings; as, "And cherubim sing anthems to shepherds from the sky." Hebrew.

2. **incarnate**—B: In human form; personified; as, "Hail the incarnate deity." Latin *incarnatus* (made flesh).

3. **exultation**—D: Great joy, especially as a result of a triumph; as, "Sing in exultation." Latin *exultare* (to leap up).

4. **Emmanuel**—B: Messiah; name given to the Savior; deliverer; as, "Jesus, our Emmanuel." Hebrew (literally, God with us).

5. **yule**—B: Christmas; the Christmas season; hence, yule log, yuletide. Old Norse *jol* (originally the name of a heathen festival to mark the winter solstice).

6. **wassail**—A: Spiced ale drunk during Christmas Eve celebrations; also, the festivities themselves; as, "Love and joy come to you, and to you your wassail too." Middle English ("be in good health").

7. **advent**—C: Arrival, specifically of Christ; hence, the period including the four Sundays before Christmas. Latin *adventus* (arrival; coming).

8. **cloven**—D: Split apart; divided in two; as, "Still through the cloven skies [the angels] came with wings unfurled." Past participle of cleave (to split or sever).

9. **laud**—C: To praise; acclaim; as, "We laud and magnify Thy glorious name." Latin *laudare*.

10. **nowel**—B: Exclamation of joy at the birth of the Savior; also, a Christmas carol; a kind of hymn. (Also spelled nowell.) Middle English from French *Noël* (Christmas).

11. **frankincense**—C: Aromatic gum resin from an African tree burned as incense; one of the gifts brought to the infant Jesus by the three Wise Men. Middle English *fraunk encens* (pure incense).

12. **natal**—D: Relating to birth; as, "Ye have seen his natal star." Latin *natalis,* from *nasci* (to be born).

13. **epiphany**—A: Sudden revelation or insight, specifically the manifestation of Christ to the Gentiles in the persons of the three Wise Men; also called the Twelfth Day. From Greek *epiphainein* (to display, reveal).

14. **deck**—A: To adorn; decorate; as, "Deck the halls with boughs of holly." Dutch *dekkan* (to cover).

15. **mirth**—B: Merriment; rejoicing accompanied by laughter; as, "Christmas fills the home with mirth." Old English *myrge* (merry).

16. **mean**—D: Shabby; low; of poor quality; as, "Why lies he in such mean estate?" Shortened form of Old English *gemæne* (common).

17. **Magi**—B: The "wise men" from the east—according to later tradition, three kings named Caspar, Melchior and Balthazar—who brought gifts to the infant Jesus. Plural of magus (one of a Persian priestly caste).

18. **firmament**—A: Sky; the heavens; as, "the spacious firmament." Latin *firmamentum* (vault of the sky).

19. **ransom**—C: To free; release from bondage or deliver from sin; as, "to ransom captive Israel." From Latin *redemptio* (redemption).

20. **nigh**—B: Close; near; as, "Stay by my cradle till morning is nigh." Middle English.

21. **waits**—D: In England, a band of street singers who perform at Christmas. Middle English *waite* (watchman).

22. **crèche**—C: A model or tableau depicting the Nativity scene, with the infant Jesus surrounded by Mary, Joseph, the Wise Men, various animals and the adoring shepherds. French.

23. **troll**—C: To sing loudly and freely; as, "troll the ancient yuletide carol." Originally, to sing the parts of a round in succession. Middle English *trollen* (to roll).

24. **sugarplum**—D: Small round candy made of flavored boiled sugar; as, "Visions of sugarplums danced in their heads."

25. **boxing day**—C: The first weekday after Christmas; a public holiday in much of the British Commonwealth. From the mid-19th century custom of giving tradespeople gifts (Christmas boxes) on this day.

26. **tidings**—D: News; information; as, "tidings of comfort and joy." Old English *tidung* (announcement, piece of news).

27. **reconciled**—B: Brought into harmony or agreement, having settled differences; as, "God and sinners reconciled." Latin *reconciliare* (to bring back together).

28. **diadem**—D: A jeweled crown worn by a sovereign; as, "Bring forth the royal diadem and crown him Lord of all." From Greek *diadein* (to bind around).

29. **manger**—C: Trough or open box for horses or cattle to eat from; as, "Away in a manger, no crib for a bed." French *mangier* (to eat).

30. **courser**—A: Swift runner, such as a horse or, in the case of St. Nicholas, reindeer; as, "So up to the house-top the coursers they flew. . . ." From Latin *currere* (to run).

Vocabulary Ratings
10-14 *Fair* **15-17** *Good* **18-20** *Excellent*

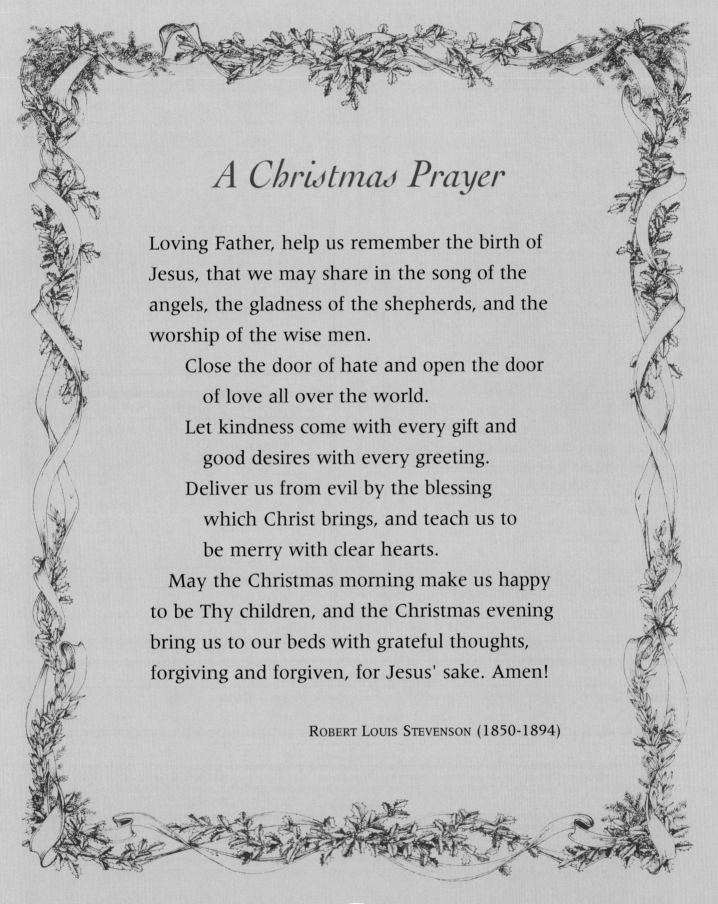

A Christmas Prayer

Loving Father, help us remember the birth of
Jesus, that we may share in the song of the
angels, the gladness of the shepherds, and the
worship of the wise men.

    Close the door of hate and open the door
    of love all over the world.
    Let kindness come with every gift and
    good desires with every greeting.
    Deliver us from evil by the blessing
    which Christ brings, and teach us to
    be merry with clear hearts.

May the Christmas morning make us happy
to be Thy children, and the Christmas evening
bring us to our beds with grateful thoughts,
forgiving and forgiven, for Jesus' sake. Amen!

ROBERT LOUIS STEVENSON (1850-1894)